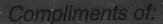

D0044454

Alan has delivered a compelling vision for investing in eternity that will reshape the way you think about your financial future. *The Eternity Portfolio* delivers fundamental truth that is powerful yet practical. I believe these principles will make a tremendous difference for all eternity as we focus our investing in God's strategic Kingdom work.

Josh McDowell
Best-selling author of **More Than a Carpenter**

I believe that one of the reasons God has blessed America is in order to fund the Great Commission. Alan Gotthardt has delivered a book full of compelling and practical strategies for how each Christian can have a financial stake in that plan. *The Eternity Portfolio* is a must-read for those who want to experience the excitement and joy that comes from investing in eternity. Don't miss out on this opportunity of a lifetime.

Larry Burkett
Founder and chairman of the board, Crown Financial Ministries

The Eternity Portfolio is a critical book. I know of no other like it. My husband and I are not only the wiser for having read it, we are filled with excitement at the prospects of God multiplying and using our resources in an even more strategic way for the furtherance of His kingdom. What could be more important? I recommend this book for every child of God, whether rich or poor.

Kay Arthur
Best-selling author and president, Precept Ministries International

When it comes to stewardship, Alan Gotthardt is on the cutting edge. *The Eternity Portfolio* has challenged and encouraged me and has confirmed how God is leading our family to be intentional about investing in eternity. This book is a "must-read" for anyone serious about their faith and their money.

Dr. Johnny M. Hunt
Senior pastor, First Baptist Church Woodstock

It has been my personal experience in life that it is better to give than to receive. *The Eternity Portfolio* reinforces this idea by providing compelling, biblically based guidance on the joys of investing in others. Enjoy the book for yourself and then share these new insights by impacting others and their eternity.

S. Truett Cathy
Founder and chairman, Chick-fil-A, Inc.

In *The Eternity Portfolio,* Alan Gotthardt has provided a terrific resource for those desiring to grow into a life of more disciplined and more biblical stewardship. The paths he outlines (in sufficient detail for personal implementation) are certain to lead those who follow them into the joy the Lord intended for participation in His Kingdom. They will also allow you to place your treasure in heaven instead of here, where most of what we have invested will not last for eternity. If you are looking for practical help now in building your own Eternity Portfolio, this book is for you.

James T. Draper, Jr.
President, LifeWay

As a church pastor for many years, I have used numerous books on stewardship and money management to instruct our people. But I do believe this is the most comprehensive and thorough work I have read. Alan has provided an extremely valuable resource for the church in this excellent work.

Randy Pope
Pastor, Perimeter Church

After reading Alan's book, I was impressed that this is a man who has something significant to say. This book is challenging and even compelling, as well as being extremely practical. I strongly recommend this book as one that can go on your bookshelf to be referred to again and again.

Ron Blue
Best-selling author and founder, Ronald Blue & Company

The Eternity Portfolio represents a paradigm shift in strategies for long term investing. Alan Gotthardt has masterfully woven together two important financial principles: investing and giving. In a remarkably simple way, he challenges us to shift our focus off of the stock market or the bottom line, and begin to invest for eternity. I recommend this book to anyone who is serious about long-term investing. What an amazing challenge to see our gifts as investments in the lives of others, investments in eternity.

Sonny Perdue
Governor, state of Georgia

I appreciate *The Eternity Portfolio*'s emphasis on the big picture. If we look at living and giving—and all we pour our lives into—through the lens of eternity, what we see is radically different. This book is thought-provoking, practical, and inspiring.

Randy Alcorn
Best-selling author of **The Treasure Principle**

The gift of giving is recognizing that we are but stewards of the resources with which we have been entrusted. It is required of a steward that he or she be found faithful. *The Eternity Portfolio* provides a helpful guide to those who seek to be wise and faithful stewards.

C. William Pollard
Chairman Emeritus, ServiceMaster

The stock market always focuses on Return on Investment. *The Eternity Portfolio* gives timeless principles for investment that keeps on giving, with returns that are unmatched. Take God at His word and watch how He'll bless a giving heart!

Robert E. Reccord
President, North American Mission Board, SBC

There is a responsibility that comes with financial blessings. And, since it all belongs to God, we should be looking for how He would have us manage it. *The Eternity Portfolio* is a well thought out plan for making the most of your finances. I believe it will help my family, along with many others, grow to new levels of faithfulness.

Coach Mark Richt
Head coach, University of Georgia Football

I wish every Christian had an Eternity Portfolio! Alan Gotthardt's solidly biblical approach gives you a step-by-step guide to making financial and giving decisions with eternal rewards in mind. Follow the principles of this book and be blessed!

Luis Palau
International evangelist

Books on stewardship and giving abound, but are seldom very original or particularly helpful. Alan Gotthardt's *The Eternity Portfolio* is the first book I have seen that actually covers new ground by telling a believer how to maximize his investment and consequently his giving to Kingdom causes. I pray that every church will gain access to this excellent work.

Dr. Paige Patterson
President, Southeastern Baptist Theological Seminary,
Wake Forest, North Carolina

This book will inspire and motivate you to become a better manager of your money. The truth here is not only that what we give and invest—if based on our values—brings incredible joy to us personally, but that our "earthly portfolio" can literally change the world (and us!) as God transforms it into an "Eternity Portfolio."

Dave Ramsey
Best-selling author and nationally syndicated radio host of
The Dave Ramsey Show

For most people, when it comes to faithfully handling money, giving is the final frontier. In *The Eternity Portfolio,* Alan combines biblical wisdom with financial strategy to create a solid plan for your giving that will change your life. It is a great book. After you read *The Eternity Portfolio,* your vision for long-term investing will never be the same.

Howard Dayton
CEO, Crown Financial Ministries
Author of **Your Money Counts**

Alan Gotthardt connects the dots in one of the most critical areas of our lives. With a total paradigm shift on creating wealth and investing with purpose, this highly devotional book is a must-read. If every church member reads and acts on this practical wisdom, our churches will never again need to beg for money and will soar in their endeavors for the Kingdom.

Jay H. Strack
President, Student Leadership University

I believe Alan has done an excellent job explaining the eternal link of how we use our God-given possessions and the eternal rewards that will come to us. My prayer is that God will use this work to further His Kingdom through generous giving.

Wesley K. Willmer
Vice president of university advancement, Biola University

While laying a solid biblical foundation for why we should give, this is a great "how to" book that shows how to formulate a true action plan for "laying up treasures in heaven" for eternity.

Hugh O. Maclellan, Jr.
President, The Maclellan Foundation

Alan Gotthardt's book has coined a phrase that I hope churches in the future will use over and over: *The Eternity Portfolio.* His sound, biblically based insights keep us focused on truly long-term investments that build up the kingdom of God.

Dr. Bryant Wright
Senior pastor, Johnson Ferry Baptist Church

Alan Gotthardt's book, *The Eternity Portfolio,* is going to make a major and positive difference in the way and the places you invest. You are going to be a whole lot more effective at it and a whole lot more pleased when you do it. Money isn't, you see, only about how you get it, it's about what you do with it. This is a book that will make a major and positive difference in your life and for the Kingdom of God. I commend it to you for both.

Steve Brown
Key Life Network

The Eternity Portfolio is a powerful, practical, biblically supported book that gets to the heart of God's purposes for stewards of His great blessings. I was particularly impressed by the new paradigm of giving presented on God's priorities for money and God's asset allocation. Alan Gotthardt has brought a fresh approach to a subject that needs new expressions.

David M. Coleman
President/CEO, Atlanta Union Mission

In a time when opportunities for excellent giving are increasing exponentially, we need to become far more *intentional* and *thoughtful* regarding how we steward what God has entrusted to us. *The Eternity Portfolio* by Alan Gotthardt will help you do just that! This book will be a key resource as you seek to make a difference, both now and for eternity. I highly commend it to you.

David Wills
President, National Christian Foundation

In the Kingdom of God, His planned eternal portfolio focuses on His most valuable investment, His only Son. Alan Gotthardt's *The Eternity Portfolio* features biblically sound, financially solid, practical strategies that maximize investing opportunities eternally in the Kingdom of God.

Mark Brister, Ph.D.
President, Oklahoma Baptist University

Thank you for *The Eternity Portfolio.* This book has challenged my thinking and my giving. You have focused the reader to think from eternity's perspective. While we will not know and understand the mystery of eternal rewards until our earthly lives are over, the thought and encouragement of how the Lord desires to multiply and bless our obedience and faithfulness clearly enriches our worship and gives us an opportunity to bring glory and joy to the Father's heart. It is my prayer that those who read this book will experience a joy and blessing in giving that is beyond their greatest expectation.

Lu Dunbar
President, Royal Treasure

Alan Gotthardt has produced a groundbreaking work that will help define the future of Christian financial planning and charity. *The Eternity Portfolio* is both practical and inspirational as it guides you towards structuring your affairs so that your life can have a meaningful impact in the only time frame that really matters—eternity. Readers are sure to be blessed with its practical insights as well as its biblical perspectives on wise investing and giving.

Rusty Leonard, CFA
CEO, Stewardship Partners Investment Counsel, LLC; Founder, Wall Watchers

The Eternity Portfolio provides dramatic insights and application in giving.

David Cavan
President & CEO, Cavan Real Estate Investments

Alan Gotthardt delivers a convincing explanation of Jesus' teaching that it is in a Christian's enlightened self-interest to be generous. Gotthardt systematically shows how to be a wise and effective investor in God's kingdom by following biblical principles. If the people of America who call ourselves "Christian" were to truly believe God's promises about money and follow His principles of wise giving, countless lives would be changed for Christ around the world.

Laurence Powell
President, Powell Family Enterprises

THE ETERNITY PORTFOLIO ∞

THE ETERNITY PORTFOLIO

ALAN GOTTHARDT

A Generous Giving book published by
Tyndale House Publishers, Inc., Wheaton, Illinois

To my wife, Melissa, a treasure that God graciously gave me before I could appreciate even a small part of its worth. Thank you for your love and your friendship on this incredible journey we make together.

Visit Tyndale's exciting Web site at www.tyndale.com

Copyright © 2003 by The Strategic Life Initiative, Inc. All rights reserved.

Author photo by Scott McIlrath. Copyright © 2003 by Alan Gotthardt.

Edited by Karin Stock Buursma

Designed by Luke Daab

Unless otherwise indicated, all Scripture quotations are taken from the New King James Version. Copyright © 1979, 1980, 1982 by Thomas Nelson, Inc. Used by permission. All rights reserved.

Scripture quotations marked NIV are taken from the *Holy Bible,* New International Version®. NIV®. Copyright © 1973, 1978, 1984 by International Bible Society. Used by permission of Zondervan Publishing House. All rights reserved.

Scripture quotations marked NASB are taken from the *New American Standard Bible,* © 1960, 1962, 1963, 1968, 1971, 1972, 1973, 1975, 1977 by The Lockman Foundation. Used by permission.

Scripture quotations marked NLT are taken from the *Holy Bible,* New Living Translation, copyright © 1996. Used by permission of Tyndale House Publishers, Inc., Wheaton, Illinois 60189. All rights reserved.

All royalties payable to the author from the sale of *The Eternity Portfolio* are being donated to The Strategic Life Initiative, Inc., a nonprofit foundation dedicated to empowering and equipping people to be more strategic and intentional in how they live and the choices they make.

Library of Congress Cataloging-in-Publication Data

Gotthardt, Alan.
  The eternity portfolio / Alan Gotthardt.
    p. cm.
  Includes bibliographical references.
    ISBN 0-8423-8435-9 (hc)
    1. Stewardship, Christian. I. Title.
    BV772 .G62 2003
    248′.6—dc21   2003004996

Printed in the United States of America

09 08 07 06 05 04 03
7   6   5   4   3   2

TABLE OF CONTENTS

What would happen if we saw giving as a way of investing? If we gave our giving "portfolio" the same attention we give our retirement portfolio? What would happen if we stopped asking, "How much do I have to give?" and started asking, "How can I invest in eternity by giving?" How would our lives change if we became aware of the rewards of faithfully investing our resources?

Alan Gotthardt asks these questions, and his answer is *The Eternity Portfolio*.

There are many books on the market about the principles of managing money and many books about why Christians should give. But Alan's thought-provoking book is unique because it combines the two concepts and takes them to the next level by including the family and ministry in the plan. In an approach that's grounded in Scripture, Alan leads you through the process of how to fund, design, implement, and monitor your Eternity Portfolio. He takes his expertise as a financial planner and applies it to the idea of radical generosity.

Alan communicates a compelling vision for the kingdom of God as the ultimate long-term investment, and he gives a step-by-step plan for how you can have a part in this incredible opportunity. With charts, graphs, income-tax and estate-planning information, detailed case studies, and reflective questions, this book is extremely practical. It provides what you need to start maximizing your investment in the kingdom of God. The tools to succeed are in your hands!

As Christians in America, we are living in a time of unprecedented wealth and luxury, yet many Christians give a smaller percentage of their income now than at any other time in history. Alan makes the case that we are missing God's perspective on investing for the long-term. The powerful message of *The Eternity Portfolio* can change lives. Think of the huge impact on ministry across the world if Christians began to invest generously for eternity!

I encourage you to read this book. Your life and your view of eternity will never be the same.

John C. Maxwell
Founder of The INJOY Group
Best-selling author of *The 21 Irrefutable Laws of Leadership*

My personal journey of faith began when I was five years old, and my faith was of the purest kind—I knew nothing else. Our family attended church faithfully, and my mother taught us the Bible before we could read or write. From an early age I heard that God existed before time began, that He hung the stars in place and spoke the world into existence. He made it all for His glory and created us in His own image to glorify Him and enjoy Him forever. But humankind rebelled against the Creator even from the beginning; our relationship with a holy, righteous God was broken by the wrong things we have done. I found out that God, in His love for the whole world, promised a Savior who would provide a way of reconciling this relationship. This Savior, Jesus Christ, lived two thousand years ago.

As a young boy, that seemed a long time ago in a galaxy far, far away. But God was calling me to Himself. As I grew older, my nature led me to dig deeper, to ask questions, to ponder and investigate the evidence of these childhood lessons.

Those who know me recognize that I have a deep desire to understand truth and then incorporate the logical implications of that truth into my life. What I have found after many years of study and observation is that God is much more than I could ever understand or imagine. He is the only thing I have found worthy of infinite worship. And the great thing is that He truly does desire us to worship Him with all of our heart, soul, body, *and mind*. God is more than a match for any sort of intellectual challenge His finite creatures can muster. All of my investigation has not replaced faith with knowledge; instead, it has confirmed faith and increased my awe of God's majesty.

The Eternity Portfolio is one of the logical extensions of the truth I have learned. God has positioned me to work daily with some of the wealthiest and most influential people in the world. Through their lives I have seen and understood vicariously the limitations of the best this world has to offer. My conclusions mirror those of the wisest and wealthiest man who ever lived—King Solomon, who recorded his thoughts in the book of Ecclesiastes. I am more convinced than ever that the only true meaning in life is achieved through a personal relationship with God through Jesus Christ, and further, the commitment of one's life passions and possessions to His designs. The result is eternal life, eternal joy, and eternal rewards. May God bless you in the pursuit.

Alan Gotthardt

ACKNOWLEDGMENTS

This book could not have been possible without the lifelong training and example of my parents, Fred and Gladys Gotthardt. Thank you, and know that whatever God chooses to do with *The Eternity Portfolio* is a return on your investment in my life. To my business partners, Chris Dardaman and Dave Polstra, I owe a debt of gratitude for your support and contributions to this work. A big thank you to everyone at Generous Giving, including Hugh O. Maclellan, Daryl Heald, and Neal Joseph, for catching the vision for this project early on and making it happen. Also to my editors at Tyndale, Jan Long Harris and Karin Buursma, who did a fantastic job on the book. Finally, to my pastor, Dr. Johnny Hunt, who has been my biggest encourager and has had a tremendous influence on my life, thank you.

A TALE OF THREE MANAGERS

There once was a wealthy man who was departing on a long journey. He was to be gone for an indefinite period of time—maybe a few years, maybe even a few decades. In preparation for this extended absence, he called together his three trusted financial managers and divided his assets between them. "Take this money and use it to further my interests," he charged each one.

The wise owner knew the abilities of each of these three managers and divided the funds accordingly. To Charlie Wise he gave $5 million, to Sarah Prudence $2 million, and to Jeffrey Short $1 million.

Confident that his affairs were in order, the owner set sail, not to be seen again for many years. Charlie and Sarah set to work immediately, laying plans for several investment ventures.

Charlie had this great idea the owner had given him about starting franchise operations of the owner's business. The owner's product was such that it really sold itself. Those who had a need for it just kept coming, and they couldn't help but introduce it to their friends and acquaintances. Charlie spent a good deal of time communicating daily with the owner via phone and e-mail. Over the years Charlie partnered with others affiliated with the owner to establish a worldwide distribution network for the product. Business was booming and the profits were really starting to accelerate when the owner returned.

Sarah spent a good deal of time studying written instructions the wealthy owner had left behind. After communicating with him on some initial strategic issues, she felt confident of the right direction for her investment. Sarah developed a marketing division for the owner's main product line that gave away free samples and promoted goodwill and interest in the owner. Sarah was in constant communication with him and was able to market his true persona very effectively. Sales really began to flow, and although Sarah's division did not see all the results directly, she knew from the company field reports that she was having a huge impact. It seemed like they were just getting started when the owner returned.

Jeffrey was really excited at the prospect of $1 million. *Look what the owner gave me!* he thought. *The world is at my disposal.* He seemed to re-call some vague instruction about the owner's interest, but Jeffrey was not much for communication, and he didn't have time to read any of the owner's written instructions. *If he is going away for such a long time, I need to earn a living,* he thought. *Who knows when or even if the owner will re-turn?* Jeffrey set aside most of the money in a safe-deposit box at the bank. He used some to start a personal business and became successful in his own right. Every now and then someone would mention to him his respon-sibility as a manager of the owner's money. Out of guilt he would put back in the safe-deposit box a little of what he was using. He figured that in a few more years there would be opportunity to focus on the owner's invest-ment. But time passed quickly, and fear struck Jeffrey's heart when he heard that the owner had returned.

Each of the managers was called in to give account for their service. "I am so glad to see you again," started the owner. "I really trusted you when I gave you my fortune to invest, and I can't wait to see how you've done."

Charlie could hardly contain his excitement. "At first I wasn't sure how your big idea would ever be successful, but the more we talked and the fur-ther things went, the more I bought in to the whole strategy." He handed over a bank statement that showed $10 million in the corporate account. "And that's just the profits we have collected," Charlie said, beaming. "It's difficult to measure the value of the whole empire!"

The owner was obviously pleased. "Well done, my friend. You have man-aged my investment faithfully for all these years. You could have enjoyed a lot of smaller pleasures along the way, but I think you'll be pleased with what is in store for you." The owner explained the new and greater responsibili-ties he had for Charlie and the enormous reward set aside for his faithfulness.

Charlie was almost speechless in his joy and gratitude, but he managed to stammer, "It seems like so much for the effort I expended . . . with *your* money."

Seeing Charlie leave the owner's office with a dazed smile on his face, Sarah was a little apprehensive. She quietly handed over the financial statements for her division, with $4 million showing on the balance sheet.

"It seems somewhat small after all these years," Sarah began. But the owner interrupted her with a wave of his hand.

"On the contrary, Sarah, you have done well. This is a good return on my investment, and yet you don't know a fraction of what has accrued to my empire as a result of your diligent efforts." Sarah was thrilled as the owner explained the vast treasure that was hers, along with a new and greater role in the company's management. "All those sacrifices along the way were duly noted, Sarah," he said. "The hours you put in, the financial commitment—none were forgotten. You made the most of my investment."

Sarah couldn't help but wonder at the seeming inequity of the whole thing. "I only did what I was instructed. . . . And in return, all this?"

Upon hearing of the owner's return, Jeffrey had scrambled to pull together the $1 million that had been entrusted to his care. It seemed so small after all these years that he had the bank give it to him in bags of fives and tens so it would look more significant. As he approached the owner, the excuses began. "Here it is, all $1 million. I knew you were a ruthless owner, and it scared me a little. So I kept your money safe in the bank, and now you can have it back."

The owner was extremely displeased to see no return on his money after so many years. "What do you mean, Jeffrey? You wicked and lazy manager!" he exclaimed. "You thought I was a ruthless owner and yet you did *nothing* to make my money grow? Even if you had deposited it in a bank account I would have earned something. I had great things planned for you. But you forfeited it all for the paltry returns of your own investments." The owner motioned to his guards. "Take the money from him and give it to Charlie Wise. And throw this worthless manager out on the street. He will never work again, and he will suffer loss forever for his mismanagement of my assets."

LIVING ON PURPOSE

Thus ends the extraordinary tale of the three managers—updated with creative license from the Parable of the Talents told by Jesus in Matthew 25:14-30. This parable represents the distilled essence of what the Bible says about our lives as managers of God's resources:

➤ We have been entrusted with money and material possessions.

➤ We should be intentional about God's plan for investing them.

➤ We will have to give an account for our management.

➤ We will be rewarded or suffer loss based on our faithfulness (or lack thereof).

Most people travel through life passively reacting to their surroundings and influences. Life just happens. Someone once said that 80 percent of success is merely showing up, and people tend to live in that fashion, giving little thought to the big picture. The Christian life, however, is meant to be lived *on purpose.* God has created us to live to His glory, and He has given us guidelines in the Bible for how that should work.

The apostle Paul writes that the true believer has died to himself and now lives *only* for the glory of God. This is a lofty standard, but if it's true, we who claim to be Christians must look for the direction God has for every aspect of our lives! Without vision and disciplined planning, we will miss out on the incredible joy, peace, and blessing that come to those who fully integrate their faith and life.

The backbone of that integration is in the area of managing our material resources. We spend most of our waking hours earning, spending, saving, maintaining, and worrying about our possessions. Because this is a primary focus of our lives, those who want to be faithful managers must seek guidance in the only standard of truth we have—the Bible. Jesus was talking about the proper use of wealth in the book of Luke when He said:

> Whoever can be trusted with very little can also be trusted with much, and whoever is dishonest with very little will also be dishonest with much. So if you have not been trustworthy in handling worldly wealth, who will trust you with true riches? (Luke 16:10-11, NIV)

As we relinquish the practical matter of finances to God's direction, we can begin to experience the abundance that He wants for each part of our lives—both in our spiritual relationship with Him and in our relationships with people. As we master the basics of faithful life management, our vision is broadened. The more we understand God's priorities for His resources and what true riches are, the more we realize that when we give, we are *investing.* Investing for His glory and our eternal reward.

This book was written to inspire your own vision for those eternal rewards and to equip you with a comprehensive strategy for making investments that last forever. Once you glimpse the future, however, there is no turning back. Since God opened my eyes to this reality, it has consumed my thinking and priorities. I have felt compelled to implement it in my own life. If you are like me, the concept of eternal rewards will be the most profound truth you will ever learn about using money.

The Eternity Portfolio is about *financial investing*. Although there are other parts of your life you can invest, such as your time and abilities, this book is about money. It is about the opportunity to commit your financial resources to something so big, so incredible you will wonder how you could have missed it until now.

The Eternity Portfolio is about *maximum-growth investing*. The strategy outlined within these pages will generate returns far above anything you ever will achieve in your brokerage account, 401(k), IRA, or personal business.

> The more we understand God's priorities for His resources and what true riches are, the more we realize that when we give, we are *investing*. Investing for His glory and our eternal reward.

The Eternity Portfolio is about *really long-term investing*. In the world of investments, *long-term* typically means greater than five years. For individuals, an investment horizon longer than thirty to forty years is unusual. The investment discussed in this book lasts much longer. In fact, this strategy will provide for your needs starting now and *literally* reaching to eternity.

Finally, *The Eternity Portfolio* is about *guaranteed investing*. An investment is only as good as the underlying asset or guarantor. For example, if you purchase a bond, that investment is only good if the issuing company is able to repay it with interest. The plan outlined in these pages is backed by the strongest guarantor with the best and longest credit rating in history. And unlike what we sometimes experience in our personal investments, the wealth of this guarantor is unaffected by stock-market fluctuations.

The strategy of the Eternity Portfolio will change the way you think about money—and it will change your life.

CHAPTER 1

Faithful Managers: Investing with Their Values

In This Chapter:

- The truth about investing
- How the faithful manager invests
- God's two purposes for money
- The investing equation

THE TRUTH ABOUT INVESTING

People often miss the point of investing money. After years of working with some of the wealthiest people in the world as a financial advisor, I have found that there are several common misconceptions. Some think of investing as a game to be won. Others see it as a goal in and of itself—to "be a successful investor." Most think of investing as a way to accumulate as much money as possible during their lifetime. Then there are a few who understand the real but hidden truth about investing—*it is a means to an end.*

Investing money is the process of committing resources in a strategic way to accomplish a specific objective. If done properly, investing will take you from where you are to where you want to go. In the financial-planning business we think of investing in terms of a person's overall financial strategy (see chart on page 2). For optimal results, each part of your financial situation should be considered in light of the whole. Investing is simply a component of the financial strategy that you must integrate with your entire plan to be effective.

Several years ago I was designing a portfolio for a newly widowed

STRATEGIC WEALTH MANAGEMENT

client who was in a unique situation. Most of Mrs. Brown's assets were in a trust that paid her the income generated each year. Since her husband's pension covered all of her modest living expenses, Mrs. Brown wanted to give away all of the income generated from the trust assets. Not only that, she wanted to *maximize* the income generated each year to be able to give away as much as possible during her lifetime. Most people in a similar situation would want to *minimize* the current income and maximize the long-term growth of the trust for the benefit of children or grandchildren many years down the road. Needless to say, the portfolio we developed for Mrs. Brown was very different from what we would typically use. Success for her was measured in a radically different way. Her life plan guided the strategy and made an impact on how she would invest her finances.

INVESTING BEGINS WITH VALUES

Money has no intrinsic value, only relative value. Its worth is measured by the ability to exchange it for something of value to the owner. In this light, the man who has no money and no wants is in the same position as one who has all the money in the world but cannot buy what he wants. In both cases, money is irrelevant because it cannot accomplish its purpose.

The point? *Investing is important only as a means of accumulating money to be exchanged for something of value to you.*

Personal core values influence everything you do, and they should be the starting point for any investment plan. Your values represent who you are and what you consider important. Many influences shape and mold your core values, including family, friends, faith, and life experiences. These values define your life and should also be the basis for managing your finances. Your investment strategy will be truly effective only to the extent that it furthers your core values.

INVESTING IS ONLY MEANINGFUL
IN TERMS OF YOUR VISION

Successful investing requires vision. You must be able to see at least a glimmer of the future rewards to understand that delayed gratification is worthwhile—that what is not spent on yourself today will be even more valuable in the years to come. When it comes to investing, vision is what turns a big spender into a big saver as retirement approaches. Vision is what enables a young couple to buy less and "eat in" more while putting aside funds for their child's college education. Vision motivates a person to give up *now* for *the future*. In a society that constantly tells us to spend and consume at a frantic pace, vision enables us to ignore the siren song of instant gratification and instead focus on the future.

But a vision of what? *Rewards.* What type of rewards? *Those that are attractive based on your values.* Values are transformed to vision as you begin to see the potential reward. Your vision encompasses the goals and objectives you have for living your core values, and it understands the payoff—the reward for achieving your objectives.

∞ |

Vision motivates a person to give up now for the future.

For example, love for family is one of my core values. I want to be around my children, be a positive influence on them, and do everything possible to ensure their well-being. Each day I grow in my understanding of what it takes to live out that core value. I have a clearer *vision* of the objectives that must be met to accomplish that. From a relational standpoint these might include eating dinner with my family each night of the week or reading Bible stories after dinner. From a financial standpoint these include such things as providing housing, food, and clothing. Saving for college educations and for retirement also become parts of the long-term vision. And I picture the rewards, such as a happy and successful family and the personal benefits of good relationships. *Expectation of rewards brings vision for achieving them.*

INVESTING IS A STRATEGIC PROCESS

As you become passionate about your vision, you develop the discipline for achieving it. As a person pursues the reward, he will make hard choices and sacrifices. Discipline is the vehicle that drives a vision to fulfillment. For example, when you're saving for retirement, discipline forces you to consider your spending patterns and invest a certain amount each month. Discipline requires a wise investment strategy that's focused on your long-term goals. It pushes you to monitor your plan and to make adjustments where needed. Discipline *creates and sustains* a good investment strategy. Shown as an equation, investing might look something like this:

Continuing our example from before, let's start with the core value of loving my family. Over the years my **vision** increases and I understand more about what it means to love them—in this example, by providing financially. As the **rewards** become clear, my desire to achieve the goal expands my vision. That vision brings with it the **discipline** to create, implement, and monitor a **wise** financial **strategy** for making it all happen.

Whether the objective is retirement, a new car, or a college education, this equation holds true. When it comes to investing, the *clarity* of your vision and the *quality* of your strategy determine the degree of your success. We'll come back to this equation throughout the book to help us remember the factors that add up to investment results.

HOW THE FAITHFUL MANAGER INVESTS

What does this mean for the Christian who desires to be a faithful manager of the resources God provides? The details will vary from person to person, but there are some common principles that form the foundation of an investment plan. The faithful manager wants to invest money with a clear vision and a quality strategy based on personal *values.* Equally important is the desire for the *rewards* of faithful management. Let's look at values, the first building block.

VISION
VALUES + EXPECTED REWARDS

VALUES

In talking to Christians over the years, I have found that faithful managers share a set of core beliefs related to their stewardship responsibilities:

1. God owns everything and controls the distribution of wealth.

In Psalm 24:1 we read, "The earth is the Lord's, and all its fullness, the world and those who dwell therein." God created everything and it all belongs to Him. Not only that, but He controls what happens to it. "Both riches and honor come from You, and You reign over all. In Your hand is power and might; in Your hand it is to make great and to give strength to all" (1 Chronicles 29:12).

A logical extension of this understanding is that God is in charge of providing everything we need. "Therefore do not worry, saying, 'What shall we eat?' or 'What shall we drink?' or 'What shall we wear?' . . . For your heavenly Father knows that you need all these things. But seek first the kingdom of God and His righteousness, and all these things shall be added to you" (Matthew 6:31-33). In his commentary on these verses, Dr. John MacArthur discusses the contrast between people of faith and those who have no hope:

> Those who have no hope in God naturally put their hope and expectations in things they can enjoy now. They have nothing to live for but the present, and their materialism is perfectly consistent with their religion. They have no God to supply their physical or their spiritual needs, their present or their eternal needs, so anything they get they must get for themselves. They are ignorant of God's supply and have no claim on it. No heavenly Father cares for them, so there is reason to worry.[1]

How different should our outlook as Christians be? Although we are to be obedient and work diligently, we know that God is ultimately in control of all the financial resources that come our way.

2. We must all give an account of our stewardship.

We are told in Ecclesiastes 12:14 that "God will bring every work into judgment, including every secret thing, whether good or evil." We know that salvation and eternal life are granted based on our faith in Jesus Christ. However, the works we do in His service will be judged on their merits and will be rewarded accordingly. "For we must all appear before the judgment seat of Christ, that each one may receive the things done in the body, according to what he has done, whether good or bad" (2 Corinthians 5:10).

> "We will be judged on the basis of our loyalty to Christ with the time, talents, and treasures that were at our disposal."
> —Erwin Lutzer

In this passage, Paul was talking about a "judgment seat" that is similar to a legal bench in a modern-day courtroom. The one major difference will be the judge. Unlike an earthly judge, the One to whom we must give account already knows everything we have or haven't done, and He will judge our motives as well as our actions. Maybe this is why when the reformer Martin Luther thought about the Judgment he said that there were only two days on his calendar: today and *that day*.

As Americans, most of us have been blessed with far more than the vast majority of all the people who have ever lived. We may find it hard to believe this because we know plenty of people who have more or earn more than we do. The fact remains that when compared to the condition of most people around the world, even lower-income Americans are considered wealthy. And, in the words of Erwin Lutzer, "We will be judged on the basis of our loyalty to Christ with the time, talents, and treasures *that were at our disposal*" (emphasis added).[2]

Most importantly, our Lord Jesus makes an observation about where we will stand in the judgment: "From everyone who has been given much, much will be demanded; and from the one who has been entrusted with much, much more will be asked" (Luke 12:48, NIV).

The coming judgment motivates us to seek God's will for every aspect of our life, including our finances. Page after page in Scripture echoes this theme of accountability.

3. Time is short; eternity is long.

Understanding the brevity of time is a hallmark of the faithful manager. "Do not boast about tomorrow, for you do not know what a day may bring forth" (Proverbs 27:1). If you are not guaranteed tomorrow, the only way to live is for today.

Planning is not wrong; on the contrary, faithfulness requires that we use God-given wisdom to prepare for the future. However, the faithful manager is not fooled into thinking he will work and save and strive for that magical day in the future when he can finally focus on God's purpose in his life. He sees the danger in putting off the responsibility to live for Christ *now*. The life abandoned to God's purpose, the life of no regrets, can only be lived with the view that each day could be our last on earth. Eternity stretches out before us.

4. The pursuit of material riches is not a valid goal in and of itself.

There is nothing wrong with having money. The Bible is full of godly men and women who were wealthy, including Abraham and Job. The question is one of purpose. Money can be spent in many ways for our personal benefit. It can buy a certain lifestyle, new houses and cars, and vacations. Eventually, however, the question becomes, "Now what?" The richest man who ever lived, Solomon, said it best:

> I denied myself nothing my eyes desired; I refused my heart no pleasure. My heart took delight in all my work, and this was the reward for all my labor. Yet when I surveyed all that my hands had done and what I had toiled to achieve, everything was meaningless, a chasing after the wind; nothing was gained under the sun. (Ecclesiastes 2:10-11, NIV)

God has gifted some people with the ability to generate money. They have become wealthy by His grace and providence. The question for them becomes, "What should I do now with His resources?" John Galsworthy puts it this way: "Wealth is a means to an end, not the end itself. As a synonym for health and happiness, it has had a fair trial and failed dismally."[3] One of life's greatest ironies is that many people spend their entire lives chasing after wealth only to find that most of the truly rewarding things in life have very little to do with money. The wealthy learn this by experience. Those who are the happiest find purpose in their work, helping others, or some other meaningful activity.

Rich or poor, the faithful manager looks to God as the owner and master, and looks to money as a means to accomplish His eternal purposes.

5. God has two objectives for money.

Scripture is an invaluable reference tool for the faithful manager since he or she wants to know as much as possible about God's plan for money. (A full discussion of all the verses on finance in the Bible is beyond the scope of this book. See Appendix D for information on some of the many good books written on the topic and visit www.GenerousGiving.org/Bible for a more complete listing of Scripture verses.) While there is more in the Bible on money and material possessions than almost any other topic, it can all be boiled down to two priorities: *invest in family* and *invest in others.* That's it. Care for your family and help others.

VISION

FINANCIAL VALUES

1. Invest in family
2. Invest in others

∞

We have now reviewed some of the values shared by faithful managers: All wealth belongs to God, we are accountable for how we use it, time is short, pursuit of riches is not a valid goal, and God wants us to invest in family and others.

Remember, in our investing equation *values* are translated into *vision* based on a desire for *rewards*. So what rewards are in view as we evaluate God's two priorities for money?

REWARDS FOR INVESTING IN FAMILY

The Bible does not say much about rewards for investing financially in family, yet most of us spend almost all of our resources in this area. Why is that?

The first reason is obvious: We face the results on a daily basis. There is a natural sense of responsibility to provide for family that is enforced by the realities of life. In other words, God does not need to tell you to feed your children; they let you know that they're hungry. However, we are reminded of this obligation in 1 Timothy 5:8: "But if anyone does not provide for his own, and especially for those of his household, he has denied the faith and is worse than an unbeliever." Paul was teaching the church how to care for the poor, and he wanted to emphasize the primary responsibility to support family members.

The second reason we readily use money for ourselves and our families is because we have a clear view of the reward. I think ahead to when my children will be independent and hopefully well-adjusted, with families of their own. I think about them receiving a good education and maybe even some inheritance when I'm gone. I have a vision of financial independence for my wife, Melissa, and me one day. Although I enjoy working in my business, there may come a time when we would like to be able to pursue other things without requiring any outside income.

The reason it is so easy for me to focus my finances in this area is that I can readily understand the rewards for investing in my family.

The obligation side of the equation keeps me going on the tough days, but it is a very real vision of the future reward that empowers me with passion to achieve the goal.

How is this desire for rewards reflected in my vision for investing? It turns my values into a road map and shows me how to get where I want to go. If you'll look at the expanded investing equation, you'll see how this plays out.

VISION		
VALUES	**GOALS**	**REWARDS**
Invest in family	Current expenses *(home, cars, etc.)*	Physical needs met
Physical needs		Good relationships
Spiritual, emotional, and mental development	Future expenses *(retirement, education)*	Spiritual vitality
	Legacy *(inheritance)*	Productive people

My experience has shown that for most people, the vision for investing in their family starts to become much clearer after about age forty. At that point, their passion (or panic, as the case may be) drives them to look for a wise financial strategy to achieve their goals. They are ready to focus on what I call the Family Portfolio. This is also what is commonly known as financial planning or managing your money.

As the name suggests, the Family Portfolio is a long-term strategy to provide money for the physical and developmental needs of the family. A definition of "needs" is very important in this process, and it should be the topic of much prayer and thoughtful consideration (more on that in chapter 4).

A great deal has been written about personal finance for Christians, and it *is* a critical part of being a faithful manager. Because our everyday lives are so complex, most people do have a general idea that they need to plan in this area. (For more information on general financial planning, see additional resources in Appendix D.)

STRATEGY
DISCIPLINE + WISDOM

Creating and executing a wise strategy starts with discipline, and discipline starts with planning. Careful planning involves understanding three things: (1) your current situation, (2) where you want to go, and (3) how to get there. Furthermore, a disciplined manager understands his or her limits and seeks out wise counsel as needed. When you formulate a strategy, all areas of the family finances need to line up with your goals.

We have talked about the vision part of the investing equation. Now let's look at how the strategy maps out:

STRATEGY

DISCIPLINE	Issues/Tools	WISDOM
Planning	Budgeting	Bible/Prayer/Holy Spirit
Communicating	Income taxes	Advisors
Spending	Loans	Experience
Saving	Business	Books and other resources
Paying off debt	Investments	
	Risk management	
	Estates & trusts	

Formulating an effective strategy is a detailed and time-consuming process. It is, however, necessary for those who seek the rewards. Keep in mind that your Family Portfolio strategy should be dynamic. Even though many pieces of the plan will remain the same over time, periodic review and adjustments are essential to the long-term health of the portfolio.

WHAT ABOUT INVESTING IN OTHERS?

Wait, we missed something. Isn't charitable giving part of my family's financial picture? Shouldn't it be included in the strategy outlined above? Well, yes and no.

At one time I thought of giving as little more than a "random act of kindness." We gave money to our church because Melissa and I were taught as children to give at least 10 percent of our income back to God. If we felt particularly moved by the needs of a family or a missionary and there was room left in our budget, we would give a little more. Over the years we donated lots of clothes and old stuff to Goodwill and put a few dollars in the Salvation Army bucket at Christmas. There was never much thought involved, and certainly no planning.

Maybe you can relate to this. If you have been a Christian for any length of time, you probably have developed some feelings about giving. Unfortunately, many people feel resentful that pastors and nonprofit organizations always seem to be asking for money. The giving that actually occurs is more often from a sense of guilt than from purpose or compassion, and it almost never involves any strategic planning. Why do you think that is true? If giving to others is one of God's two main purposes for money, why is that not lived out in the life of the average Christian? Could it be that we don't understand that this is an investment? Could it be that we don't understand the rewards?

We'll investigate this further in the next chapter.

CHAPTER 1
Faithful Managers: Investing with Their Values

DISCUSSION QUESTIONS

Note: The questions at the end of each chapter are intended to help you think through the ideas that have been raised and build your own Eternity Portfolio. Generous Giving, a nonprofit ministry dedicated to good stewardship, has created a Web site, www.EternityPortfolio.com, that can help facilitate this process on-line and allow you to track your Eternity Portfolio over time.

1. How do you react to this statement: "God has a plan for your life, *including your money,* and you will be held accountable for faithfulness to His plan"?

2. In today's society, what does a faithful manager look like? How does he or she live within American culture?

3. What values drive your thinking and actions in the areas of possessions, family, working, investing, and giving? Is there a disconnect between what you know to be the "correct" answers and the way you are actually living?

4. Consider the idea that investing is only a means to an end and that *all* of our earthly goals are truly short-term in light of eternity. How does that impact your financial priorities?

5. How important is it to you to invest in your family?

6. What are your views on giving and investing in others? Have you spent any time studying what the Bible says about giving? How can you be more intentional in this area of your life?

CHAPTER 2
The Ultimate Investment

In This Chapter:

■ Investing in others: obligation or opportunity?

■ Eternal rewards—now and to come

■ Should a Christian seek eternal rewards?

■ Giving as the ultimate investment

Twenty-seven years is all it took. After reading the Bible since 1975 and studying and working as a financial advisor for over a decade, it came to me: Giving is the ultimate long-term investment. It just made sense. Investment returns well above what could ever be found else-where, no risk of default, returns compounded *forever,* benefits to be enjoyed even more *after* this life . . . wow! It may have taken me a while to catch on, but now the idea had my attention.

But wait a minute. We ended the previous chapter by asking why people are not motivated to invest in others by *giving.* If giving is the ultimate investment, why are so few people motivated by it?

INVESTING IN OTHERS: OBLIGATION OR OPPORTUNITY?

In chapter 1 we noted that God has two priorities for money: investing in family and investing in others. Most of us have a pretty good handle on the first one. For me and for many others, the confusion came into play with the "investing in others" part. Why? Two reasons. First, I did not realize the priority God places on giving. Second, I had never understood the opportunity for rewards.

ALIGNING WITH GOD'S PRIORITIES

I had always seen giving as a *part of my Family Portfolio*. In other words, giving was in the same category as paying off the mortgage, paying the utilities, educating my children, and saving for the future. The picture looked something like this:

GOD'S PRIORITIES FOR MONEY?

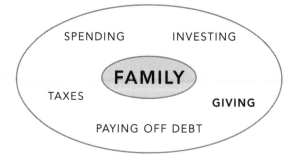

SPENDING   INVESTING

FAMILY

TAXES

GIVING

PAYING OFF DEBT

After studying the issue in depth, however, I have come to realize that giving is actually a separate category, consistent with the top-level priority God places on money. This new paradigm of giving is more accurately represented as:

GOD'S PRIORITIES FOR MONEY

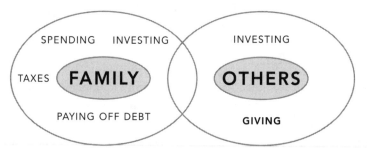

SPENDING INVESTING   INVESTING

TAXES **FAMILY**   **OTHERS**

PAYING OFF DEBT   **GIVING**

Therefore, I believe that there are two parts to a person's financial situation—the Family Portfolio and the Eternity Portfolio. Although interrelated, each is distinctive in its focus.

OBLIGATION OR OPPORTUNITY?

The second problem with my view on giving was that I didn't see the opportunity for rewards. Instead, I saw giving as taking away money that could be spent on me or my family. It was hard to get real excited about that.

Most of what I have read and heard about giving portrays it as the *obligation* of every Christian. That is accurate at one level, since much of what is said in the Bible about giving conveys a message of responsibility.

I feel the obligation to give based on at least three realities in my life. First, I give out of a sense of gratitude for what God has done for me and how He has provided for my needs. Second, I give to show my love for God in worship of Him. Third, I give as a tangible fulfillment of my responsibility to love other people, to help provide for their needs. Each of these is a biblical obligation. According to the Bible, these sacrifices are pleasing to God. Hebrews 13:16 is a great example of this: "But do not forget to do good and to share, for with such sacrifices God is well pleased."

However, there is something much bigger that makes me passionate about my giving as an *opportunity*. Much of what is written about giving in Scripture speaks about the upside, the reward for those who give to help others. There is very little in the Bible about rewards for investing for yourself and your family. Why is that? Is giving more important in God's eyes than meeting my family's needs? I don't think so. The answer lies within human nature.

Earlier we asked why giving is not a priority for most Christians. *The answer is that obligation alone is not enough to give us a* **vision** *for investing in others.*

What was it in our investing equation that transformed values to vision? *The desire for rewards.* God knew that with few exceptions the

Family Portfolio would take care of itself because we can see the rewards. He also knew that we are sinful humans, and unless He specifically told us there would be rewards for being generous to others, the thought might not even cross our minds. So He inspired the writers of Scripture to say a great deal about the rewards for giving.

God wants us to take this second priority for money just as seriously as the first. He wants to change our hearts and give us a desire for the personal rewards of investing in others.

Why do we need a change of heart? Remember that vision for investing starts with our values, which show most clearly what is important to us. Dr. Bruce Wilkinson once said that the things you do are directly connected to where your heart is, as if by a rubber band. Although you can make temporary adjustments where your actions move away from your heart, after a time they always snap back. Any true life change must begin with a heart change.

How does a change of heart in the area of giving come about? It starts with faith and believing God. As the Scripture verse says, "Faith comes by hearing, and hearing by the word of God" (Romans 10:17). Life change takes heart change, which takes faith, which takes hearing the Word! In this particular passage Paul was referring specifically to faith in Jesus Christ as Savior; however, faith is equally applicable as we try to develop a vision for the proper use of our possessions. The writer of Hebrews describes this "temporal versus eternal" perspective as Moses viewed it:

> By faith Moses, when he had grown up, refused to be known as the son of Pharaoh's daughter. He chose to be mistreated along with the people of God rather than to enjoy the pleasures of sin for a short time. He regarded disgrace for the sake of Christ as of greater value than the treasures of Egypt, because he was looking ahead to his reward. (Hebrews 11:24-26, NIV, emphasis added)

So the faith of Moses gave him the vision for the *reward*, which he viewed as more valuable than all the treasures of ancient Egypt! Our faith, and therefore our vision, comes by hearing what God has written about the incredible opportunity of giving.

ETERNAL REWARDS—NOW AND TO COME

We defined the *values* of the faithful manager in the first chapter, but what about the *rewards?* The Bible is full of God's promises to His faithful children. Rewards both now and forever are in store for those who love and obey Him. Perhaps more surprisingly, the Bible teaches that Christians can *increase or decrease* eternal rewards based on their faithfulness in life.

VISION
VALUES + EXPECTED REWARDS

In his book *Your Eternal Rewards,* Erwin Lutzer writes, "The person you are today will determine the rewards you will receive tomorrow. Those who are pleasing to Christ will be generously rewarded; those who are not pleasing to Him will receive negative consequences and a lesser reward. In other words, your life *here* will impact your life *there* forever."[4]

Nowhere in Scripture is the connection between our actions in this life and eternal rewards more clearly described than in the area of giving. Over and over the case is made that those who are generous with this world's resources will be blessed of God both in this life and in all eternity. Let's look at a sample of what the Bible says about rewards for giving.

In the words of Solomon, the wisest man who ever lived:

Honor the Lord with your possessions, and with the firstfruits of all your increase; so your barns will be filled with plenty, and your vats will overflow with new wine. (Proverbs 3:9-10)

It is possible to give freely and become more wealthy, but those who are stingy will lose everything. The generous prosper and are satisfied; those who refresh others will themselves be refreshed. (Proverbs 11:24-25, NLT)

He who has a generous eye will be blessed, for he gives of his bread to the poor. (Proverbs 22:9)

In the words of Paul, who wrote much of the New Testament:

Remember this: Whoever sows sparingly will also reap sparingly, and whoever sows generously will also reap generously. Each man should give what he has decided in his heart to give, not reluctantly or under compulsion, for God loves a cheerful giver. And God is able to make all grace abound to you, so that in all things at all times, having all that you need, you will abound in every good work. As it is written: "He has scattered abroad his gifts to the poor; his righteousness endures forever."

Now he who supplies seed to the sower and bread for food will also supply and increase your store of seed and will enlarge the harvest of your righteousness. You will be made rich in every way so that you can be generous on every occasion, and through us your generosity will result in thanksgiving to God. (2 Corinthians 9:6-11, NIV)

And, in the words of Jesus Christ Himself:

Everyone who has given up houses or brothers or sisters or father or mother or children or property, for my sake, will receive a hundred times as much in return and will have eternal life. (Matthew 19:29, NLT)

Give, and it will be given to you: good measure, pressed down, shaken together, and running over will be put into your bosom. For with the same measure that you use, it will be measured back to you. (Luke 6:38)

These represent just a handful of the many biblical references, but do you get the sense that God wants to encourage giving? If we look specifically for the rewards promised in Scripture, we will be amazed at just how many there are.

WHAT ARE ETERNAL REWARDS?

First and foremost let me say that nothing in this book should be construed to advocate the so-called "prosperity theology" of giving. God has not promised to give you a Lexus, a beach house, or an easy retirement if you are faithful in giving. He has not even promised to reward you *in this lifetime*. Although it is abundantly clear that we will be rewarded based on our faithfulness, what is not as clear is exactly what the *nature* and *timing* of those rewards will be.

| ∞

From a timing standpoint, we need to realize that our life on earth is only a fraction of our eternal existence.

From a timing standpoint, we need to realize that our life on earth is only a fraction of our eternal existence. Think of examples such as the beggar Lazarus in the Bible (Luke 16:19-31) and the martyred saints described in Hebrews 11 who never received their reward in life. However, there are also many examples in Scripture of God's current blessings. Much of the reward for giving that was promised in the Old Testament related to increased crops and herds as well as protection from enemies—all of which related to physical rewards during life on earth.

My personal experience has convinced me that God can certainly choose to bless faithful giving during this life. Many others would agree. Listen to the testimony of a minister who lived in England in the 1600s:

I dare challenge all the world to give me one instance, or at least any considerable number of instances of any truly merciful men, whose charity has undone them. But as living wells the more they are drawn, the more freely they spring and flow: so the substance of liberal men doth oftentimes, if not, ordinarily, multiply in the very distribution: even as the five loaves and few fishes did multiply in their distribution by the hands of the Redeemer. And the widow's oil increased by pouring it out for the holy prophet.
—Reverend Thomas Gouge[5]

Reverend Gouge personally lived out this testimony as he funded his own ministry as well as many poor people in his area using the estate left by his father.

So God can choose to bless our giving in this world with increased material possessions. But what if He does not? Most of the verses about eternal rewards do not mention money or material possessions as rewards for giving. Instead, they mention rewards in heaven. These seem to fall into three main categories:

➤ **Crowns**—"Now there is in store for me the crown of righteousness, which the Lord, the righteous Judge, will award to me on that day—and not only to me, but also to all who have longed for his appearing" (2 Timothy 4:8, NIV). See also James 1:12, 1 Peter 5:4, and Revelation 2:10.

➤ **Treasure**—"Provide purses for yourselves that will not wear out, a treasure in heaven that will not be exhausted, where no thief comes near and no moth destroys" (Luke 12:33, NIV). See also Matthew 6:20, Mark 10:21, 1 Timothy 6:19.

➤ **Positions of authority**—"If we endure, we will also reign with him" (2 Timothy 2:12, NIV). Also see Matthew 19:28 and Revelation 3:21.

Without question, the rewards for Christians who are faithful in this life will be great. *This includes faithfulness with their material possessions.*

Several great books on eternity and eternal rewards are available (see Appendix D for a list). Though we will not know for sure what each of these rewards will be like until we get to heaven, the emphasis placed on obtaining them should make us excited about the prospect.

IS IT SELFISH FOR A CHRISTIAN TO SEEK ETERNAL REWARDS?

Should a Christian pursue God's favor and the prospect of being rewarded? Does that seem self-serving and maybe even covetous?

It is certainly possible to have wrong motives related to giving—or anything else we do as Christians, for that matter. This gives rise to what Paul refers to as "wood, hay, and straw" that will be burned at the judgment (1 Corinthians 3:8-15). However, Paul also talked a great deal about striving to obtain a crown, and he encouraged the early church to do the same.

This is not about obtaining heaven and eternal life. Paul was clear in his writings that salvation is by faith alone. Crowns and other rewards result from our actions here on earth. The fact is that our best interests are aligned with God's purpose and plan for our lives. Randy Alcorn puts it this way in his book *In Light of Eternity:*

> Though God's glory is the highest and ultimate reason for any course of action, Scripture sees no contradiction between God's eternal glory and our eternal good. On the contrary, glorifying God will always result in our greatest eternal good. Likewise, pursuing our eternal good—as he commands us to—will always glorify God.[6]

THE ULTIMATE INVESTMENT

If there are rewards to be had for all eternity from giving, and seeking eternal rewards is not in conflict with God's will for us, shouldn't we be looking to give as much as possible? Doesn't this sound like a significant investment opportunity? Compared to the other investments we can make during our lifetime, which might produce rewards for thirty to forty years, the concept of eternal rewards is pretty compelling.

∞ |

Possessions compete for our affections, taking our heart away from God.

Does Scripture provide a mandate for maximizing this ultimate investment opportunity? Apparently the apostle Paul thought so. As he raised money for the work of Christ in the first-century churches, he had in mind the investment return to the giver. Notice his words to the Philippian church:

> And you yourselves also know, Philippians, that at the first preaching of the gospel, after I departed from Macedonia, no church shared with me in the matter of giving and receiving but you alone; for even in Thessalonica you sent a gift more than once for my needs. Not that I seek the gift itself, but I seek for the profit which increases to your account. (Philippians 4:15-17, NASB, emphasis added)

Paul had just told the Philippians that he had learned to be content in any situation, and he goes on to say that he has everything he needs. His concern was for the givers. As they gave to further the kingdom of God, something happened: *profit increased to their account.* What account is that?

Before we draw conclusions, let's look at some instructions Paul sends to Timothy for the church at Ephesus:

> Command those who are rich in this present age not to be haughty, nor to trust in uncertain riches but in the living God, who gives us richly all things to enjoy. Let them do good, that they be rich in good works, ready to give, willing to share, storing up for themselves a good foundation for the time to come, that they may lay hold on eternal life. (1 Timothy 6:17-19)

First, we should understand that to be "rich" in those days meant that you had the bare essentials—food, clothing, shelter. So most of us would be included. Also note that there is nothing inherently wrong with being rich because God "gives us richly all things to enjoy." However, these people were advised to be abundant in good works for the purpose of storing up a foundation for themselves! MacArthur's Commentary interprets the original language this way:

> By sharing their earthly treasures with others, they are **storing up for themselves the treasure of a good foundation for the future.** Apothesaurizo **(storing up)** could be translated "amassing a treasure," while themelios **(foundation)** can refer to a fund. The rich are not to be concerned with getting a return on their investment in this life. Those who lay up treasure in heaven will be content to wait to receive their dividends in the future when they reach heaven.[7]

So Paul gives specific instructions to the Christians at Ephesus to give in order to accumulate eternal rewards. Where do you think Paul got the idea? He got it from Jesus Christ Himself. Many years before Paul even became a Christian, Jesus was preaching to the multitudes and said these words:

> Do not lay up for yourselves treasures on earth, where moth and rust destroy and where thieves break in and steal; but lay up for yourselves treasures in heaven, where neither moth nor rust destroys and where thieves do not break in and steal. For where your treasure is, there your heart will be also. (Matthew 6:19-21)

Possessions compete for our affections, taking our heart away from God. What was Jesus' command? Do not lay up treasures? No. As Bruce Wilkinson has noted, Jesus was not saying it is wrong to lay up treasures. He was making the case that it is just not smart to accumulate them where they will be destroyed. Even if we save them from robbers, rust, and insects, we will leave everything here when we die.

Jesus was telling us to "lay up for [ourselves]," to get a stake in the ultimate financial investment.

The message from Scripture is clear. Jesus gives the options: suffering loss by holding on to our possessions, or gaining an incorruptible inheritance by giving them away. These verses, combined with many others, lead to an astonishing but unavoidable conclusion: We have the ability to influence our eternity in heaven based on the faithful use of money on earth, specifically in the area of giving.

Jonathan Edwards, one of the most famous American preachers of the eighteenth century, said it like this:

> What man, acting wisely and considerately, would concern himself much about laying up in store in such a world as this, and would not rather neglect this world, and let it go to them that would take it, and apply all his heart and strength to lay up treasure in heaven, and to press on to that world of love?[8]

How does this fit into our investing equation? We are beginning to get a vision for the rewards of investing in eternity. When I'm investing financially for my family, my primary motivation is the *tangible reward* such as providing physical needs or education. When it comes to investing financially in others, my primary motivation is *eternal rewards*. It's interesting to note that the rewards that motivate me to invest in family seem to be the *means* of achieving the rewards in giving to others. (See the chart on page 29.) We should see no conflict between what God wants us to be about in life (loving others) and the rewards for being faithful to the task.

Lack of vision, not greed, is probably the main reason most of us accumulate and spend in this world instead of laying up treasure in heaven. God has appealed to our own enlightened self-interest by promising eternal rewards in the area of giving, in effect making it the ultimate investment. This kind of approach benefits God's kingdom purposes and accrues to our ultimate good.

Once we catch the vision, the questions start: Does the Bible really offer guidance on strategic giving? How much should I give, or better

VISION		
VALUES	**GOALS**	**REWARDS**
Invest in family	**Current expenses** *(home, cars, etc.)*	Physical needs met
Physical needs		Good relationships
Spiritual, emotional, and mental development	**Future expenses** *(retirement, education)*	Spiritual vitality
	Legacy *(inheritance)*	Productive people
Invest in others	Physical needs met	ETERNAL REWARDS
Physical needs	Good relationships	• Treasures in heaven
Spiritual, emotional, and mental development	Spiritual vitality	• Crowns
	Productive people	• Positions of authority

yet, how much should I keep? How much is enough for my family? How do I choose where to give? Will my gifts be used effectively for the kingdom? How can I involve my family in this strategy and teach my children to give generously?

What we need is a strategy, a plan that will empower us to be faithful managers.

We need the Eternity Portfolio.

CHAPTER 2
The Ultimate Investment

DISCUSSION QUESTIONS

1. How do you think of giving—as obligation or opportunity? What is that based on? How would God have you look at it?

2. Do you believe that God rewards Christians who are faithful with the time, abilities, and possessions He entrusts to their care? Can we earn rewards?

3. Can a Christian lose rewards because of unfaithfulness in this life?

4. Have you ever thought about the nature of eternity, heaven, and eternal rewards? What passages in the Bible have shaped your thinking in this area?

5. Why do you believe it is difficult for Christians today to focus on eternity and laying up treasures in heaven as opposed to this world?

6. Are you open to the possibility that God may have a plan for you to give more than you ever thought you could or would? How would He communicate that to you? How would you accomplish it?

CHAPTER 3

The Eternity Portfolio

In This Chapter:

- The virtues of being intentional
- Biblical guidance for successful giving
- Overview of the Eternity Portfolio strategy

Several years ago I began to notice an unusual similarity between my work with traditional investment portfolios and the strategy I had prepared for another area of my personal finances—giving. Eventually I realized that the principles were almost completely interchangeable.

As a result, my family has begun to view our giving as investing. The churches, ministries, and individuals we support make up our "Eternity Portfolio" of kingdom investments. The Bible is our guide for maximizing that portfolio.

The unique paradox of the Eternity Portfolio is that instead of saving and accumulating money, we are actively trying to give it away to God's glory, to follow Christ's teaching to "lay up treasures in heaven." As Pastor John MacArthur explains:

> It is possible that both our treasures on earth and our treasures in heaven can involve money and other material things. Possessions that are wisely, lovingly, willingly, and generously used for Kingdom purposes can be a means of accumulating heavenly possessions. When they are hoarded and stored, however, they

> *not only become a spiritual hindrance but are subject to loss*
> *through moth, rust, and thieves.*[9]

Although giving is certainly not the only way of achieving rewards in heaven, it does seem to be the only logical way of *investing money* for the really long term. The Eternity Portfolio is a personal strategy for being intentional about investing financial resources in those things that generate eternal treasure in heaven.

THE VIRTUES OF BEING INTENTIONAL

In the past, my wife, Melissa, and I spent very little time thinking about our giving strategy. We made donations in reaction to opportunities (or obligations!), with little planning or accountability. Often we justified this "spontaneity" by saying that giving should be done "as the Spirit leads."

As we began to view our giving more seriously, I started thinking. No one would argue that financial planning for family finances is unspiritual. In fact, I tell folks all the time that it is just prudent stewardship. In our churches we plan everything from the Sunday school strategy to airplane reservations for mission trips. Is that unspiritual? Of course not. Hear the words of Reverend Samuel Harris written over 150 years ago on the matter of systematic giving:

> *System always promotes efficiency. What would become of a man's*
> *worldly business, if he managed it without system, never executing*
> *a plan or making an investment till solicited, and abandoning labor*
> *to the control of impulse or convenience? And can he hope for any*
> *better results from a like disregard of system as a steward of God?*
> *From such lack of order, what but embarrassment and failure can*
> *result to the enterprises of benevolence? And what shall we say of*
> *those professors of Christ's religion who show so thorough an*
> *understanding of the necessity of system in worldly business, so*
> *utter a neglect of it in their contributions to benevolence: who are*
> *full of forethought and anxious calculation to realize the utmost of*

*worldly acquisition; deliberate and farsighted in planning, cautious
in executing, lynx-eyed to discern an opportunity of gain, exact to
the last fraction in their accounts, but heedless and planless in all
they do for charity? Verily, "the children of this world are wiser in
their generation than the children of light"; but "the children of
light" show no lack of that wisdom, till they come to use property
for the benefit of others than themselves.*[10]

Jesus encouraged His disciples to be shrewd in using wealth as a
means to achieve heavenly goals (Luke 16:1-12). The book of Proverbs speaks of the benefits of planning, wise counsel, and diligence in
managing life. It seems clear that the Christian life is a balance of prudent planning and faith. And in my experience, there are at least four
major benefits to having a strategic plan for your giving.

1. Planning maximizes giving—and leads to more effective giving.

Lack of clarity is the enemy of investing. There is nothing like viewing
your retirement plan in the cold light of day to get you motivated to
invest. Seeing the numbers on paper highlights the difference between where you are financially and where you want to be. The same
is true in giving. Once you start to formulate goals and measure results, your momentum builds, allowing you to discover ways to give
more than you ever thought possible.

Planning also brings accountability. As the investor, you not only
have expectations of yourself but you also look more closely at the effectiveness of the organizations you're investing in.

2. Planning makes it easier to say no.

This may sound strange in light of the theme of this book, but being
able to say no is one of the most freeing concepts you can learn. Without a giving plan, you can easily feel guilty whenever you have an opportunity to make a donation. "Should I be doing more?" "I haven't
given anything to them in a while." "It *is* a really good cause." Some-

times you don't think you should give but you don't feel right saying no either.

I want to be open to spontaneous giving opportunities as the Lord leads me. However, when we have prayerfully and thoughtfully planned where the majority of our giving should be invested, we can honestly and freely tell someone that we are fully committed in that area and cannot help at this time.

3. Planning makes you a cheerful giver.

Each day you are confronted with the lure of instant gratification. There is seemingly no end to the ways you can use your money to fulfill a desire you have *right now*. Investing is not easy; it takes discipline to set aside money for the long term. A giving plan forces you to make that decision ahead of time so you don't have to make it a thousand times each month. This is why 401(k) plans and other automated savings plans are so effective. The participants understand that those funds are not available for spending and learn to manage their budgets accordingly.

Those who plan their giving no longer have to decide whether to give or spend each time an opportunity is presented. They are energized and joyful when looking for investments because the money is already designated; it is no longer available for living expenses. The question then becomes: "Should I invest in this *particular* opportunity, and if so, how much?" Each day the habits of earning, spending, and saving money are reinforced in your life. Strategic planning makes your giving a habit as well.

You should determine beforehand how much you will give, then investigate opportunities God brings to invest those resources. Paul taught this to the early church (see 2 Corinthians 9:6-7). The Christians in Jerusalem were suffering because of famine and poverty, and Paul asked the Gentile churches to contribute to a fund he would deliver to the church in Jerusalem. He realized that if the Corinthians did not plan their gifts ahead, they would make other commitments with the resources and be resentful when he came to receive their gift. Cheerful giving results from planning.

4. Planning helps you understand where faith begins.

Although some would tell you that it takes faith to give away *anything*, most of us realize we have a certain level of discretionary income that can be given without much sacrifice or faith. As a result of prudent planning, we gain a new sensitivity to the amount of giving that will test our faith and to the idea of needing to be constantly dependent on God.

I hope you see some of the benefits that result from planning your giving. Building your Eternity Portfolio is not a rigid process but an individual plan based on prayer, Scripture, and God's leading. It will be different for each family and will most certainly change over time. As a start, God has given us principles in Scripture that apply to giving, and He has provided intellect, sound reasoning, and faith to work out the details. We should start our plan by looking at the basics of successful giving as taught in the Bible.

BIBLICAL GUIDANCE FOR SUCCESSFUL GIVING

When it comes to managing your finances, it has been said that there are three main principles for success: *spend less than you earn, avoid debt,* and *save for the future.* Those three principles embody the accumulated wisdom of the ages for financial success. These are not rules that you *must* obey. Calamity will not necessarily befall you for breaking them. However, over time, these principles lead to the *greater reward.* In other words, you may finish the race without them, but you probably won't place in the top ten.

> ## STRATEGY
> ### DISCIPLINE + WISDOM

Likewise, when it comes to investing for eternity, God has given us principles that help us achieve the greater reward. The writings of the apostle Paul give us most of the guidance in this area, and he emphasizes two main themes: motives and methods.

MOTIVES

The overwhelming theme of the Bible is God's love for us and the way we should respond to that love—both to Him and to others. The way we handle our money is no exception. Paul speaks to the heart of the matter as he gives instruction to the church at Corinth:

And now, brothers, we want you to know about the grace that God has given the Macedonian churches. Out of the most severe trial, their overflowing joy and their extreme poverty welled up in rich generosity. For I testify that they gave as much as they were able, and even beyond their ability. Entirely on their own, *they urgently pleaded with us for the privilege of sharing in this service to the saints. And they did not do as we expected, but* they gave themselves first to the Lord and then to us in keeping with God's will. *So we urged Titus, since he had earlier made a beginning, to bring also to completion this act of grace on your part. But just as you excel in everything—in faith, in speech, in knowledge, in complete earnestness and in your love for us—see that you also* excel in this grace of giving.

I am not commanding you, but I want to test the sincerity of your love by comparing it with the earnestness of others. *For you know the grace of our Lord Jesus Christ, that though he was rich, yet for your sakes he became poor, so that you through his poverty might become rich.*

And here is my advice about what is best for you in this matter: Last year you were the first not only to give but also to have the desire to do so. Now finish the work, so that your eager willingness to do it may be matched by your completion of it, according to your means. For if the willingness *is there, the gift is acceptable according to what one has, not according to what he does not have.* (2 Corinthians 8:1-12, NIV, emphasis added)

So I thought it necessary to urge the brothers to visit you in advance and finish the arrangements for the generous gift you had promised. Then it will be ready as a generous gift, not as one grudgingly given.

Remember this: Whoever sows sparingly will also reap sparingly, and whoever sows generously will also reap generously. Each man should give what he has decided in his heart to give, not reluctantly or under compulsion, for God loves a cheerful giver. (2 Corinthians 9:5-7, NIV, emphasis added)

Paul speaks of a heart that is given first to the Lord and then to others. As Jesus Christ changes your heart, He changes your desires. One of those desires is to help others through giving freely. Notice how, by the grace of God, the poor Macedonians pleaded to make an investment in the kingdom that was beyond what they could afford.

> Those who "give" with selfish motives have not really "given" at all. They have merely made a purchase, exchanging a charitable deed for the praise of men. |∞

This is not to say that giving out of obligation cannot be used of God in the life of the Christian. Giving that starts as a discipline, out of simple obedience, may over time be converted to cheerful willingness, and that is when the reward is maximized.

Motive is more important to God than amount. Even if we lack the ability to give a large amount, God judges motives when it comes to reward. "For if there is first *a willing mind*, it is accepted according to what one has, and not according to what he does not have" (2 Corinthians 8:12, emphasis added). Our overriding motives for giving should be a loving response to Christ's love for us and a tangible expression of our love for others.

In the Sermon on the Mount, Jesus taught what should *not* be the motive for our giving:

Take heed that you do not do your charitable deeds before men, to be seen by them. Otherwise you have no reward from your

Father in heaven. Therefore, when you do a charitable deed, do not sound a trumpet before you as the hypocrites do in the synagogues and in the streets, that they may have glory from men. Assuredly, I say to you, they have their reward. But when you do a charitable deed, do not let your left hand know what your right hand is doing, that your charitable deed may be in secret; and your Father who sees in secret will Himself reward you openly.
(Matthew 6:1-4)

Note that Jesus is prompting us to the greater reward—the reward from the Father. Those who "give" with selfish motives have not really "given" at all. They have merely made a *purchase,* exchanging a charitable deed for the praise of men. If pride is the motivation behind our giving, we are making a purchase, not investing for the greater reward.

METHODS

When it comes to methods for giving, there are as many variations as there are Christians. However, according to Scripture, giving is to be *systematic, proportionate,* and *generous.* No passage sums it up better than this brief statement to the Corinthians.

Now concerning the collection for the saints, as I have given orders to the churches of Galatia, so you must do also: On the first day of the week let each one of you lay something aside, storing up as he may prosper, that there be no collections when I come.
(1 Corinthians 16:1-2)

We have already discussed the merits of planning and being intentional about your giving strategy. Paul's instructions were to lay something aside systematically, on a *regular basis.* He knew that if the Corinthians did not plan ahead, what little amount they would give when he arrived would be done grudgingly and out of obligation.

"Storing up as he may prosper," or, in the New International Version, "in keeping with his income" seems to indicate that successful giving should be *in proportion* as God has blessed. This is further indi-cated in Jesus' observation of the widow's offering recorded in Mark 12:41-44. Jesus emphasized to His disciples that even though the widow gave only two pennies, she gave proportionately more than the others because it represented her whole livelihood.

> *We should have a regular and proportionate plan for our ongoing investment, but at times we will be led to make extraordinary investments in opportunities that God reveals.* | ∞

One other principle to keep in mind about the methods for giving is the element of spontaneity. We should have a regular and proportion-ate plan for our ongoing investment, but at times we will be led to make extraordinary investments in opportunities that God reveals. These can be some of the most satisfying and exciting investments of all.

So there we have it—the general principles for building an Eternity Portfolio. If I were asked the secret to investing money for eternal re-wards, I could sum it up no better than the following quote:

The Law of Charity
"And this law of charity lays itself on men in all varieties of condition, with an admirable equality of pressure. It requires each to give according to his means, and according to his own judgment, formed with an enlightened conscience and a benevolent heart." —Rev. Parsons Cooke[11]

Giving should be motivated by love; be done regularly, cheerfully, and discreetly; and be done in proportion to your wealth.

OVERVIEW OF THE ETERNITY PORTFOLIO STRATEGY

Now that we've reviewed some of the biblical principles behind money and giving, we'll move from the theoretical to the practical.

The following chapters will guide you through the process of funding, designing, investing, and monitoring your own Eternity Portfolio. The material will answer the question of "How?" at the most practical level.

This strategy is intended to be a general guideline, but it is specific enough to be useful to anyone who has the desire and patience to customize it to his or her own personal situation. This is obviously not the only way to go about the process of charitable giving. What is important is that those who desire to invest in eternity develop *some* strategy to accomplish the goal.

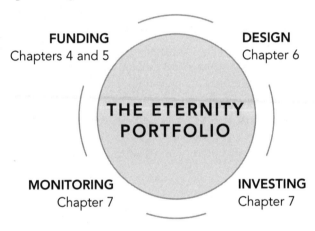

FUNDING
Chapters 4 and 5

DESIGN
Chapter 6

THE ETERNITY PORTFOLIO

MONITORING
Chapter 7

INVESTING
Chapter 7

FUNDING THE PORTFOLIO

We'll lay the financial groundwork and cover the question of "How much is enough?" from three distinct viewpoints. I'll address different methods of calculating annual giving and will introduce case studies to illustrate the process in action.

DESIGNING THE PORTFOLIO

Once you have established the funding for the portfolio, you have to plan how to give it away. The Eternity Portfolio is designed to be diversified across what I would identify as the major priorities listed in the Bible—evangelism, discipleship, and mercy. Each of these major categories has subcategories. We will discuss how I came up with these categories, some ideas for determining what percentage of the portfolio should be allocated to each area, and when to consider "overweighting" a particular category.

INVESTING THE PORTFOLIO

Once you decide the categories to be represented, the hard decisions really begin. We have to make actual investment selections among the thousands of charities in existence, and these investments should not be made haphazardly. I'll recommend guidelines that will help you find and screen appropriate candidates. This process combines prayer, the leading of the Holy Spirit, and God-given principles for effective ministry and accountability. The result is the faithful management of your Eternity Portfolio.

MONITORING AND ONGOING DUE DILIGENCE

A large part of success in any endeavor is formalizing goals, objectives, and guidelines in written form. Traditionally, an investment portfolio includes a written investment policy statement detailing how the portfolio will be managed. In much the same way, we want to document the process for managing the Eternity Portfolio. We'll discuss the key ingredients of a successful policy statement, including the mission statement, funding strategy, investment selection, and due diligence requirements.

PLANNING FOR THE FUTURE

Once you have your Eternity Portfolio functioning, you'll need to look to the future. We'll examine several effective ways you can leave both a living legacy and a financial legacy, and we'll discuss specific techniques for advanced philanthropy. Finally, we'll look at the seven golden keys for honoring God and creating maximum leverage through our giving.

As we look once again at our investing equation, we have outlined the *vision* based on values and desire for rewards. Now in the chapters ahead we'll add to that a *strategy* based on discipline and biblical wisdom—and we'll be on our way to successful investment.

THE ETERNITY PORTFOLIO

VISION

VALUES	GOALS	REWARDS
Invest in others	Physical needs met	ETERNAL REWARDS
Physical needs	Good relationships	• Treasures in heaven
Spiritual, emotional, and mental development	Spiritual vitality	• Crowns
	Productive people	• Positions of authority

STRATEGY

DISCIPLINE	Issues/Tools	WISDOM
Planning	How much is enough?	Bible/Prayer/Holy Spirit
Communicating	Taxes	Advisors
Distributing	Legacy	Experience
Saving	Due diligence	Books and other resources
	Investments	
	Giving strategy	
	Charitable trusts	

CHAPTER 3
The Eternity Portfolio

DISCUSSION QUESTIONS

1. Are you intentional about your responsibilities as a manager of God's resources? If not, why not?

2. What are some things that motivate you to give? Have you ever given with selfish motives?

3. In the past, how have you gone about the process of deciding when to give, where to give, and how much to give? In what ways would you like to change that process?

4. During childhood, most of us learned about money either through the teaching or example of our parents. Which of these "money lessons" from your parents have carried over into your adult years, specifically related to giving?

As you begin the practical work of building your Eternity Portfolio, remember that the on-line tool at www.EternityPortfolio.com can help you with this process.

CHAPTER 4

Funding the Portfolio PART ONE:
How Much Is Enough for Now?

In This Chapter:

- How much to give or how much to keep?
- Exponential generosity
- Determining how much is enough for now
- Ten thousand percent investment returns

One of my clients came to me while she was working for a successful technology company. As one of the company's first employees, her hard work had been rewarded with stock options that at one point were worth millions of dollars. Before coming to see me she had sold some of her stock to achieve a little investment diversification and had paid cash for her new home. But most of her assets were concentrated in the company stock. Then the stock market crash of 2000–2002 struck with all its fury. Especially hard hit were the technology companies, even those with solid businesses such as the one where my client was employed. Over that period of months the value of her stock and options fell by more than 75 percent.

When she came to me, we began to talk about the future and what amount of assets she would need to provide for her family's financial independence. She was dismayed to realize that she had already passed that level *twice*, once on the way up and then again on the way down. I remember what she said to me because, unfortunately, I've heard it before: "Alan, if I had only come sooner, if I had only known *how much is enough,* I would have sold more stock and secured my family's financial independence."

It was not greed that kept this woman from achieving her goals, but a lack of understanding of the finish line. In investing as well as life, understanding the end goal and knowing the right questions to ask can make or break your strategy.

When it comes to giving, your perspective drives the questions. If you consider giving primarily a duty, the question tends to be *"How much is enough giving* to fulfill my obligation and keep me from feeling guilty?" However, if you believe that giving is really the ultimate investment, the question becomes *"How much is enough for me and my family* so that I can maximize my giving?"

No matter how you calculate it, there is a fundamental, inverse relationship between how much you spend and how much you can give. In other words, more of one means less of the other. God has blessed each of us with a certain amount of resources. Those resources, according to Scripture, are for two purposes: family and others. Once we have prayerfully determined how much is needed to provide for family, the balance can be invested in others for the greater long-term reward.

HOW MUCH SHOULD I GIVE?

The starting line for building the Eternity Portfolio is funding. How much will you set aside this year to invest in others?

There are different methods for determining this amount. Most of us are familiar with the "tithe," or giving 10 percent of our gross income. Another method is to begin each year with a specific amount or percentage in mind as the target.

As long as the process integrates the biblical principles for giving (proper motives, systematic, proportionate, generous), there is no one "right" amount or method for everyone. However, as you consider how much you can give, think about the traditional investments you are making. How have you decided what should be invested there?

Take retirement savings, for instance. Retirement comes up in almost every financial-planning conversation I have. "How will this spending decision affect my retirement?" "Can we save a little more here or there to put more in retirement?" The list goes on and on. Typically, once someone understands the benefits of investing for retirement, he or she begins to look for opportunities to invest as much as possible.

Why is this particular investment so close to our hearts? Retirement is by far the most important and most long-term investment vision people have. It is the ultimate "end game" of earthly planning. To an extent, this is as it should be. As you get older, your ability to work and earn a living can be hampered by health and other issues. Wisely saving for the future is a characteristic of the faithful manager.

In the same way, once we realize the benefits of giving, we should be looking for every opportunity to invest in our Eternity Portfolio. The first step is to prayerfully and thoughtfully establish the funding requirements for our Family Portfolio. When we do that, the balance will be freed up for the investment with the greatest long-term potential—the Eternity Portfolio. We are then in a position to be used by God as a pipeline for His resources to bless others. I call this the "exponential generosity" method of funding.

Be forewarned: Exponential generosity is not for the timid or the faint of heart. It faces daily challenges from the thriving strains of the "keeping up with the Joneses" and "getting ahead in this world" viruses that constantly try to reassert themselves as financial priorities in our lives. Whether you're ready for this funding method depends largely on your vision of the rewards of investing.

EXPONENTIAL GENEROSITY

Exponential generosity is based on the supposition that at some level of financial blessing, it is no longer about me, and the future rewards from giving are far more valuable than the gratification of current spending. In other words, as God "overflows my cup" financially, I stop looking for a bigger cup and allow the blessings to flow to others.

Wealth is not a bad thing, nor is enjoying some of that wealth

As God "overflows my cup" financially, I stop looking for a bigger cup and allow the blessings to flow to others.

wrong. Scripture says that God "gives us richly all things to enjoy" (1 Timothy 6:17). However, if I enjoy everything now, I forfeit my future rewards.

Exponential generosity divides your financial resources into the Family Portfolio and the Eternity Portfolio. It takes into account what you need to spend and save to provide for current and future family needs. The balance can be invested for all eternity.

Obviously each individual situation will be different. God has strategically placed Christians in all walks of life and at all economic levels. He knows exactly what financial resources you need to live the life He intends, and that level will probably not be the same for you as it is for others.

I've included several fictitious case studies in this book that will provide practical examples for some of the concepts we discuss. All of the case studies are included in Appendix A, but we'll look at them individually in more detail in the next several chapters. Let's look now at one example of how exponential generosity might work.

∞

Donna Rutherford is forty-seven years old and works for United Package Company in Minneapolis, Minnesota. Her current salary and bonus total $74,000 per year. Donna has been saving for retirement since she started work at age twenty-three, and she owns a nice home about thirty miles outside of Minneapolis. Donna has developed the funding schedule on the next page for her Eternity Portfolio; this table allows for a simple calculation of how much she should give each year.

For example, Donna's current income is $74,000. Based on the table, she would give $2,500 on the first $25,000 (10 percent); $3,750 on the next $25,000 (15 percent); and then $6,000 on the remaining

$24,000 (25 percent) for a total of $12,250 in giving for the year. Notice that her formula is applied from the first dollar she earns.

DONNA RUTHERFORD EXPONENTIAL GENEROSITY	
INCOME	**GIVING PERCENTAGE**
$0–25,000	10 %
$25,001–50,000	15 %
$50,001–100,000	25 %
$100,001–150,000	30 %
$150,001–up	50 %

Donna's family expenses and savings get $22,500 of the first $25,000 (90 percent); $21,250 of the next $25,000 (85 percent); and $18,000 of the remaining $24,000 (75 percent) for a total of $61,750. The results look something like this:

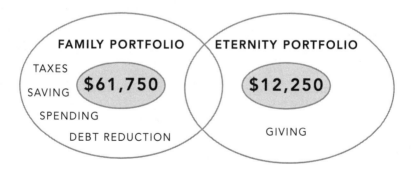

This is one example of a giving schedule. Appendix A details five case studies, and each family has a different funding calculation. It is my hope that these examples will give you some ideas regarding your own situation.

HOW IT WORKS

Before we discuss the obvious question of how to develop your own schedule, we should make some practical observations about how exponential generosity works.

First, this method of giving is *systematic*. We have not yet determined the "where" or "when" of our giving process, but the "how much" question is being answered. Donna has a portfolio of $12,250 that she has determined proactively not to spend on herself but to invest for the benefit of others. Note that the plan is not meant to exclude spontaneous giving. Certainly Donna will also have opportunities where she is led to give additional amounts, but the systematic plan serves as a foundation.

Second, this method is *proportionate* because as one makes more money, a larger percentage of each additional dollar is given away. This reflects the belief that as our needs are met, we can make a larger investment in meeting the needs of others. Donna has, in effect, set a limit on her living expenses. If you look again at her giving schedule you'll see that for income over $150,000, Donna will have only a small amount left to spend after giving and taxes.

Finally, exponential generosity *keeps our money motives pure*. If we have a plan for giving away a large portion of any additional money we earn, our priorities are simplified. A balanced perspective for the kingdom of God, not greed, becomes the only motivation to make more money.

An interesting side benefit of exponential generosity is that over time you build in a significant "downside protection." If Donna loses her job or experiences a large cut in pay, she will be living so far within her means that the blow will be much less painful.

As I was researching the idea of exponential giving, it surprised me to find examples of people throughout history who used this very system to determine how much to give. Look at this example from the 1800s:

Hence the propriety of a rule adopted by Mr. N. R. Cobb, a merchant of Boston: to give from the outset one quarter of the net *profits of his business; should he ever be worth $20,000, to give one half of the net profits; if worth $30,000, to give three quarters; and if ever worth $50,000, to give all the profits. This resolution he kept till his death, at the age of 36, when he had already acquired $50,000, and was giving all his profits.*[12]

This system has also been used in more recent times by men and women who want to maximize their investment in eternity. An example is R. G. LeTourneau, a brilliant inventor and businessman of the twentieth century who gave away 90 percent of his earnings and lived on the balance.

A proactive strategy is the best way to position yourself according to this passage in the Psalms: "If riches increase, do not set your heart on them" (Psalm 62:10). There is a tremendous freedom that comes from knowing you are going to give away a larger and larger piece of that next dollar. You have not set your heart upon it, so whether or not God will bring more wealth your way does not concern you anymore.

In order to develop a customized exponential generosity schedule, you need to answer two foundational questions:

1. How much is enough for *now?* (current living expenses)
2. How much is enough for *good?* (future living expenses)

Before you can answer these questions, it is important to have a good understanding of your current financial situation, including a cash-flow statement, balance sheet, and a listing of your current insurance coverages. We'll describe the basic elements in the following pages.

HOW MUCH IS ENOUGH FOR NOW?

Start right where you are. Take out a piece of paper and list your income and expenses. Don't spend too much time trying to make it exact right now; just get a sense for the round numbers. Use a format similar to the Annual Cash Flow Statement shown on page 54. If you are the

ANNUAL CASH FLOW STATEMENT

INCOME

Salary/bonuses	_____
Interest & dividends	_____
Retirement income	_____
Rents	_____
_____	_____
_____	_____
_____	_____
TOTAL INCOME	_____

EXPENSES

Mortgage/rent	_____
Property taxes	_____
Food	_____
Clothes	_____
Auto	_____
Recreation	_____
Income taxes	_____
Insurance	_____
_____	_____
_____	_____
TOTAL EXPENSES	_____

CASH FOR INVESTING _____
(Income – Expenses)

INVESTMENTS

Eternity Portfolio	_____
Retirement plans	_____
Other investments	_____
College funds	_____
TOTAL INVESTMENTS	_____

EXCESS CASH FLOW _____
(Cash for Investing – Total Investments)

organized type, print out a cash-flow report from your Quicken, Microsoft Money, or other computer software, and use the data to set up your Annual Cash Flow Statement. Notice that your current giving should be listed under "Investments (Eternity Portfolio)."

The point of this exercise is to see how much you are currently investing in all core areas of your finances, including your giving. This may take some time, but the result will probably be enlightening. If the "Cash for Investing" number is negative (in other words, if your current expenses are greater than your current income), you have another problem: You are living above your means. I suggest you immediately address this issue through prayer and godly counsel. Refer to the resources on debt in Appendix D and check with your local church to see if they have a financial-counseling ministry or can refer you to one. While you work out the shortfall, I would still strongly recommend that you start your investment in the Eternity Portfolio. I have heard many stories of people in that exact situation who started giving and found their way out of the financial crisis much sooner than expected.

Let's look at some major items on the cash-flow worksheet. Each of these is a key element in your financial plan, and all of these elements together affect your giving strategy. If you're a faithful manager in all areas of your finances, you'll be able to be more deliberate in your giving.

RISK MANAGEMENT (INSURANCE)

One of the areas most often overlooked when it comes to reviewing cash flow is managing risk through insurance. This is probably because we have difficulty understanding the tangible benefits for the dollars spent. Until your house burns down or you have an automobile accident, you don't realize the value of insurance. And when it comes to life insurance, the value is only received once you're dead! No wonder most people are underinsured.

From a purely financial standpoint, insurance is a cost-effective means of transferring the risk of catastrophic expenses to an insurance company. Proper financial management requires appropriate insurance

INSURANCE
PROPERTY AND CASUALTY Home Cars Excess liability Personal property
HEALTH Accident/sickness Long-term care Life
INCOME Disability

coverage. The table above shows some of the areas that should be reviewed with an experienced insurance agent. Part of the reason most people avoid buying insurance is because they do not understand it and feel vulnerable to being taken advantage of. Educate yourself before making decisions in this area, but do not avoid the decision.

Adequate insurance coverage is foundational for the faithful manager. It lays the groundwork and protects the Family Portfolio against risks.

INCOME TAXES

The largest nondiscretionary expense you have is income tax. Without proper planning (and sometimes even with it) federal and state income taxes can consume *over half* of the income you generate. Most people are not quite in that highest tax bracket, but when you include Social Security and Medicare taxes, the total could easily be 30 to 40 percent of your taxable income. Although Scripture is clear that we are obligated to pay our taxes, as faithful managers we are only obligated to pay the minimum required. This should be an area of particular attention in your planning, especially as it relates to your charitable giving.

For those who itemize deductions on their tax return, charitable giving is one of only a handful of truly tax-advantaged investments you can make. Each dollar you give to a qualified charity reduces your taxable income by a dollar.* As your taxable income goes down, your taxes go down. For example, if you are in the 15 percent income-tax bracket, you would save fifteen cents in taxes for each dollar you give. The government, in effect, pays 15 percent of your gift. Think of the savings if you are in a high tax bracket and your combined federal and state tax rate is 45 percent. Due to the tax savings, you actually pay only fifty-five cents on the dollar for each gift to charity!

The benefits can be even more attractive if you give away stock or other capital assets that have increased in value over the years. If you sell these, you will have to pay tax on the capital gains. However, if you give the appreciated assets, you do not pay tax on the gain, and, generally, neither does the charity.

> **Example:** Jeff Broward owns five hundred shares of Coca-Cola stock worth $20,000. He purchased these shares fifteen years ago for $2,000, so Jeff has what is called a "capital gain" of $18,000. He wants to make a contribution of $20,000 to his church. He could use cash, but he is considering gifting these shares. If he sells the shares for himself, the tax would be $3,600, so the cash value of the stock to Jeff is really $16,400 ($20,000 minus the $3,600 tax).
>
> Which should he give? Whether he gives cash or stock, the church gets $20,000. If he gives the cash, Jeff is left with stock worth $16,400 to him (due to the capital gain tax payable upon sale). If he gives the stock, he has $20,000 in cash left. Jeff gives the stock.

The opportunity to eliminate a capital gain and future tax down the road is pretty compelling. If you are considering this type of transaction, be sure to consult an experienced tax advisor to make sure all the details are executed properly. Incidentally, most large churches and

---

*Assuming no adjusted gross income (AGI) limitation on itemized deductions.

ministries have brokerage accounts in place and can help facilitate this type of transaction.

As you move into more advanced charitable-giving strategies, you need to take certain limitations into consideration. To generalize, these rules limit the amount of your income that can be offset each year by charitable contributions. You can deduct up to 50 percent of your income in any one year for gifts of cash to public charities. Contributions over that amount can be carried forward and used as deductions on your tax return in later years for up to five years.

> **Example:** Michelle Johnson earned $40,000 this year. She also received an inheritance of $35,000 upon the death of her grandmother. Michelle wants to make cash donations totaling $25,000 to her church and a homeless shelter in the area. Due to the income limitation, Michelle will be able to deduct $20,000 of her donations on her tax return this year ($40,000 income multiplied by 50 percent). The remaining $5,000 charitable contribution will be carried forward to be used in her tax return next year.

One final note on the tax impact of investing in the Eternity Portfolio: *Taxes should not drive or control your investment strategy.* In the traditional investing arena, the overall after-tax economic result is what is important. Minimizing your taxes is not *the* goal but a means to the goal. As a faithful manager, you should not overlook the tax benefit of giving, and you should take steps to make optimal use of the tax system. However, there will be times when gifts should be made that are not tax deductible. It is the eternal reward that must be in view, not simply income-tax savings.

OTHER LIVING EXPENSES

Lifestyle is a very personal decision and calling. God has placed us in a specific moment in time at a specific place for a specific purpose. He does not have a "Christian standard of living" that is applied across the board. What is considered a necessity in one culture might be the

| ∞

"We should travel light and live simply; our enemy is not possessions, but excess." —John Stott

height of luxury in another. Sacrifice is relative. We need to find the proper balance between living today and preparing for tomorrow (and that really long tomorrow!). I am reminded of Jesus' words to the disciples:

> And do not seek what you should eat or what you should drink, nor have an anxious mind. For all these things the nations of the world seek after, and your Father knows that you need these things. But seek the kingdom of God, and all these things shall be added to you. (Luke 12:29-31)

Our Father knows all the things we need, and He will provide. Our job is to be faithful managers and evaluate all spending decisions as spiritual decisions. You must make the final choice as to how you will allocate the money you receive. Remember: the money you spend on yourself is money you don't have available to give. *The challenge is to learn contentment so that at whatever place you are, you have enough.*

I have been amazed to see in my own life and through consulting with my clients that spending almost always keeps up with income. Whether someone makes $20,000 or $2,000,000 per year, there is no shortage of creative ways to spend it. We must learn contentment if we are going to maximize our investments, and one way to learn it is to limit the "spending" category by preprogrammed investing in other areas, be that for college, retirement, giving, short-term needs, or building up an emergency cash reserve.

Most of us have the opportunity to have a certain amount automatically deducted from our paychecks and invested in our retirement accounts. We do not consider that amount in our spending decisions because it is "off-limits." We need to do the same thing with our giving.

I recommend that you start with the cash-flow statement on page 54 and try to determine what level of spending is enough for now. Look ahead several years into the future and make some calculations. In the coming pages we will discuss in detail some of the issues surrounding your investments, but remember the goal: *Position yourself so that God can channel His resources through you to be invested for maximum return in your Eternity Portfolio.*

After you set some limits on spending, the next question is where and how much to invest, for both the Family Portfolio and the Eternity Portfolio. As you plan your approach for the future, I would encourage you to invest at least 10 percent in your Eternity Portfolio. You may not be able to get to 10 percent at this point, but set that as an initial target. It gets much more interesting than that, but the important thing is to start *somewhere.*

INVESTING FOR RETIREMENT

The ultimate investment for the Family Portfolio is saving for retirement. It is only prudent during the prime working years to save money for the future, when earnings may be more limited. The issue then becomes balancing your retirement savings with other goals. How much should you be putting aside for retirement?

Each situation is different. A lot depends on how old you are, how much you have already saved, what type of work you do, and what it will cost to retire at the standard of living you choose. The irony is that even if you nail down all those factors, you still have no idea how the future will turn out. It may be that due to market conditions you end up with much more than you need (or much less). The cost of living can change dramatically over twenty to thirty years of retirement. Deteriorating health could make retirement much more expensive or much less (if you pass away earlier than expected). The fact is, some things are out of our control. Our faith will be tested even if we take all the wise steps necessary to prepare for retirement.

We must be careful, however, not to ignore the other priorities in life by focusing solely on saving for retirement. Notice this in the parable Jesus taught about a certain rich man who seemed to be prepared:

> Then he said to them, "Watch out! Be on your guard against all kinds of greed; a man's life does not consist in the abundance of his possessions."
>
> And he told them this parable: "The ground of a certain rich man produced a good crop. He thought to himself, 'What shall I do? I have no place to store my crops.'
>
> "Then he said, 'This is what I'll do. I will tear down my barns and build bigger ones, and there I will store all my grain and my goods. And I'll say to myself, "You have plenty of good things laid up for many years. Take life easy; eat, drink and be merry."'
>
> "But God said to him, 'You fool! This very night your life will be demanded from you. Then who will get what you have prepared for yourself?'
>
> "This is how it will be with anyone who stores up things for himself but is not rich toward God." (Luke 12:15-21, NIV)

This teaching comes immediately before Jesus talks about how the Father will provide for all our needs and that we should focus on laying up treasure in heaven. What do we take from that? Is it wrong to save for retirement? No. However, we must not focus so much on saving for retirement that we neglect other, more important areas of investing, such as our Eternity Portfolio. We are not guaranteed tomorrow, much less twenty years from now, so we need to be investing for several different goals and time horizons simultaneously.

So what does a balanced approach to investing look like?

Here's one example. We met Donna Rutherford earlier when discussing exponential generosity. Now let's look at her scheduled retirement savings. Donna is now forty-seven, so she is investing 15 percent of her annual income for retirement. She is contributing the maximum amount possible to her company's 401(k) plan and then saving the balance in other investment accounts earmarked for retirement.

DONNA RUTHERFORD	
RETIREMENT FUNDING	
AGES	**INVEST**
47–55	15 %
56–67	12 %

The case studies in Appendix A illustrate five different plans for systematically saving for retirement. None of them should be considered the "best" way. They are simply examples of how different people have taken a thoughtful approach to saving. For some helpful ideas, look for the one that comes closest to your particular situation.

You will notice that in each case study there are three critical factors that significantly impact the results of retirement savings. First is the *systematic plan.* Year in and year out money is being invested on a regular basis. Second is the *element of time.* When it comes to saving for retirement, time is either the savior or destroyer depending on where you are in the process. At age twenty-five the tolerance for error in your retirement program is quite high—assuming you get started, it is hard to mess up. However, once you hit age forty, that tolerance for error begins to narrow considerably. Over age fifty you need to be putting the final touches on a well-executed plan. It is never too late to start, but you must have realistic expectations of what can be accomplished in a short amount of time.

The third major factor in investing for retirement is *achieving a certain level of growth over time.* In each of the case studies the growth rate is assumed to average 7 percent annually. That 7 percent will not, however, come in a straight line. The average takes into account that there will be years of 5, 10, and 20 percent growth as well as years of 5, 10, and 20 percent *decline,* and everything in between.

We will discuss some basics of a successful retirement investment strategy in chapter 5, but for now, understand that you need consistent growth over time to maximize your retirement savings.

INVESTING FOR COLLEGE

At one time a college education was considered a *luxury* that few could afford. Today a college education is a *necessity* few can afford. Tuition and related costs continue to rise even as new and revolutionary methods of saving for college sprout up on an almost-annual basis. Fortunately there are a growing number of federal and state scholarship plans available to offset some of these costs. However, college funding remains a significant challenge for both parents and students.

We need to clarify priorities. Saving for college is not nearly the same priority level as saving for retirement. Providing a four-year degree for your children, while important, is not as important as making sure you don't have to move in with them when you turn sixty-five because your retirement funds run out! Keep in mind that college is not out of reach for those without the financial backing of their parents. Scholarships, loans, grants, work studies—the list goes on and on, but the point is that college is accessible even for those who must pay some or all of their own way.

If you have significant financial resources, the amount you need to save for college can be estimated and put aside rather easily. This information is widely available on Web sites such as www.savingforcollege.com. You can look at the average costs for different types of schools (i.e., public, private, elite) and plug in details such as the number of years until your children start college, the amount of savings you already have, and how much you are setting aside each month. This on-line calculator will increase the tuition cost at 5 to 7 percent inflation per year until your children start college and then give you the amount you need to have set aside by the time they get there. It will also take the present value of that total, assuming a certain growth rate, and show you what you need to invest today.

The problem for most people is that, depending on how many children they have and where they will go to school, that amount can be simply out of reach. In college funding, as in retirement savings, we need balance and we need to face the realities of what can be accomplished.

In Case Study 2 (page 167), we see that John and Sheila Patterson have a college plan that is simple but effective. They have two children, ages six and four. John and Sheila have a combined income of $58,000 this year and are investing 4 percent each year toward their children's college education. They recognize that the kids will probably need some additional assistance through financial aid, jobs, and so forth, but John and Sheila feel that 4 percent achieves a balance in the family's priorities.

Contrast this with Todd and Emily Fleming (Case Study 3, page 171) who, through the sale of their business, were able to invest a lump sum of $275,000 for college funding.

Once you decide how much to invest for college savings, you then choose between the many different investment plans. Savingforcollege.com gives the pros and cons of the alternatives, including everything from savings bonds to the new and improving "529 plans." 529 plans have become the college savings vehicle of choice because they allow large and small contributions, tax-free investment earnings, and the flexibility to change beneficiaries as needed. Also, 529 plans can be used at any accredited college (including Christian colleges and universities).

Educating your children is a priority. How you pay for that, especially at the college level and beyond, is a personal decision and should be guided by your economic situation. The earlier you begin to plan and save, however, the more options you will have.

INVESTING IN THE ETERNITY PORTFOLIO

Now we come to the annual investment in the Eternity Portfolio. This is the amount that is set aside each year for your giving strategy. As a baseline measurement, we will start this investment at 10 percent of total income. We then need to determine both when and how much our giving can be increased.

First we need to get an idea of where this additional investment comes from. Let's assume that you are saving 15 percent of your annual income for retirement, 6 percent for your children or grandchildren's education, and 10 percent for your Eternity Portfolio. (For purposes of this comparison, income taxes are included with living expenses.) Depending on your annual income, the chart below shows the percentage invested in each category:

PERCENTAGE INVESTING

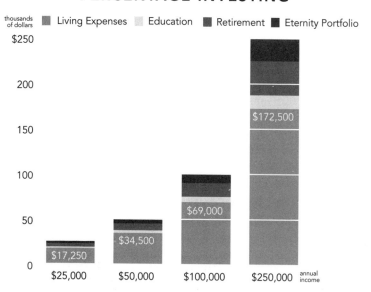

The same amount of investment, from a percentage standpoint, is made at each income level (a total of 31 percent, including funds for retirement, college, and the Eternity Portfolio). Note that even though the same percentages are invested in each category at each income level, the absolute dollar amount left over for living expenses increases substantially as income increases.

By setting in place a tiered exponential-generosity schedule, we can allow for some increase in living expenses as needed while contributing a greater percentage of each additional dollar earned. As an example, remember the giving schedule for Donna Rutherford (shown on page 66). You may never reach the income levels shown on this sched-

ETERNITY PORTFOLIO
INVESTMENT SCHEDULE

INCOME	GIVING PERCENTAGE
$0–25,000	10 %
$25,001–50,000	15 %
$50,001–100,000	25 %
$100,001–150,000	30 %
$150,001–up	50 %

ule, but make up one that fits your particular situation. The key is to figure out where you will be able to level off your living expenses so that giving can increase. As you make this decision, remember to seek the Lord's leading. His guidance is essential if we are to follow His will in our giving.

EXPONENTIAL INVESTING

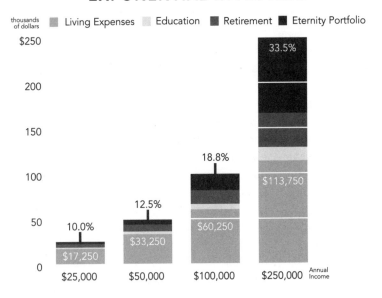

thousands of dollars — ■ Living Expenses ▨ Education ■ Retirement ■ Eternity Portfolio

Don't be surprised if you start having more to give than you ever expected. The chart on the bottom of page 66 shows how Donna's giving schedule operates at the various income levels.

Do you see the difference? As the overall income increases, living expenses start to flatten out and giving increases exponentially. As opposed to a flat 10 percent of income, Donna is investing a growing *percentage* of her income as God provides it. Also, once she achieves shorter-term investment goals, such as education funding, there will be additional amounts freed up for giving.

As you might imagine, investing with a schedule like this creates the potential for enormous lifetime results. Take the Patterson family, for example (Case Study 2, page 167). John and Sheila are in their early thirties and have established a similar tiered giving schedule for their Eternity Portfolio. Their combined annual income is $58,000. This year the Pattersons will give a little over $6,000. They will also contribute $2,000 or so for their children's education funds and invest 10 percent of their income for retirement. John and Sheila expect their income to increase modestly for inflation over the coming years.

How much can the Pattersons invest for eternity over their lifetimes? Can they really make a difference? The answer is a resounding *yes*. Projecting into the future, they will invest *$1.6 million* in God's kingdom during their lifetime! (See chart on page 68.) This is a staggering figure, representing more than ten years of their highest earnings. It makes a difference when you have a strategy and apply it consistently over time.

Think of the needs this money will meet. Feeding the hungry, spreading the Good News, teaching and discipling people around the world—all through the investment of one couple. Starting early and giving consistently as God blesses them with increase, John and Sheila will give away substantially more than they keep for themselves. At the same time, they are providing for current living expenses as well as saving for education and for their own retirement.

But what about investment returns? This chart shows only the dollars invested in the Eternity Portfolio. If we are laying up treasure in heaven, our investments will compound over all eternity. Remember the words of Jesus when He talked about the rewards of making sacrifices and following Him?

> *Everyone who has left houses or brothers or sisters or father or mother or wife or children or lands, for My name's sake, shall receive a* hundredfold, *and inherit eternal life.* (Matthew 19:29, emphasis added)

Wow! What does a "hundredfold" look like? Setting aside annual compounding, what if we just received rewards equal to one hundred times what we invested? So, for example, if we invested $20,000 for eternity over our lifetime, a "hundredfold" return on investment would grow that number to $2,000,000. That's 10,000 percent in investment returns!

That little dark strip at the bottom of the chart on page 69 is the actual amount invested. Do you get a sense for the magnitude here? Ten

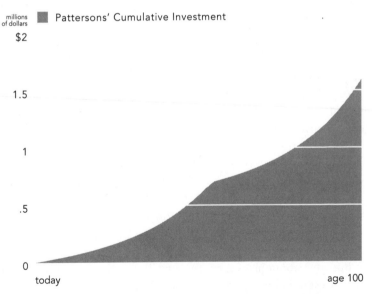

A LIFETIME OF INVESTING IN THE ETERNITY PORTFOLIO

thousand percent is a lot of growth. And this chart only covers the Pattersons' *lifetime.*

Okay, I realize that Jesus was speaking symbolically. We may not have this gigantic pile of rewards in heaven. Chances are that the eternal rewards we receive will be vastly different from anything we can imagine. However, even speaking symbolically, it still sounds like the rewards will be incredible and will be exponentially more than our investment in God's kingdom while we are here on earth.

TIME TO GET STARTED

I hope this chapter has helped you start thinking about your annual investment in the Eternity Portfolio. The point is to have a systematic way of deciding how much to invest, just as you would with any traditional investment. Throughout the process you should focus on *hearing from God* as to the amount and timing of your investment in the

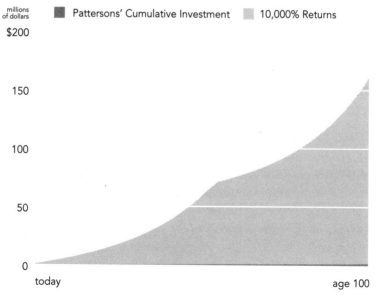

10,000 PERCENT RETURNS?

Eternity Portfolio. Diligent, intentional planning honors God but should never be a substitute for prayer and seeking His will for your giving.

∞ | *Diligent, intentional planning honors God but never be a substitute for prayer and seeking His will for your giving.*

A friend of mine named Steve, who works for the Coca-Cola Company, told me that God had impressed on him the idea of paying off his home so he and his family could be in a position to give away the amount of their mortgage payment each month. After an extended time of prayer and studying the Bible, Steve and his wife sold their Coca-Cola stock and paid off the mortgage. This was in 1998, just as the price of Coke stock was reaching its all-time high. Shortly thereafter the stock price dropped over 40 percent! Thanks to God's timing, Steve sold his stock at the peak, paid off their mortgage, and has had the freedom to invest many thousands of dollars in his Eternity Portfolio ever since.

Will something like that happen to you? Maybe not exactly, but you'll want to seek God's direction as it relates to the amount and timing of your giving.

Let's return to one other question that was posed at the beginning of the chapter. Will there come a time in your life when all other investment goals (including financial independence) have been accomplished? What then? Is that the time you can begin to focus even more on your eternal investments? More people than ever before are facing the question "How much is enough *for good?*" We'll take a look at this question in the next chapter.

CHAPTER 4:

Funding the Portfolio Part 1: How Much Is Enough for Now?

DISCUSSION QUESTIONS

1. Do you have a financial plan for your Family Portfolio? Based on the information in this chapter, how faithful do you think you are being with your money in this area?

2. Have you ever considered the idea of establishing a limit on your family's expenses over time? What would be some of the benefits of such a limit? What would be the downside?

3. What percentage of your current income is scheduled to be invested in your Eternity Portfolio? (Based on your current budget or the Annual Cash Flow Statement on page 54.)

4. Do you expect your income to increase, decrease, or stay the same over the next ten years? Who controls that?

5. How do you plan to be more intentional about your investment in the Eternity Portfolio over the next ten years?

6. How could you take greater advantage of the tax-savings opportunities in your giving (e.g., gifts of appreciated stock)?

CHAPTER 5

Funding the Portfolio PART TWO:
How Much Is Enough for Good?

In This Chapter:

- The importance of financial finish lines
- What is financial independence for Christians?
- Calculating "How much is enough?"
- What happens if I cross the finish line?

One of the hardest concepts to convey to clients is that they have crossed the "finish line" of financial independence. This is natural when you consider that for thirty or forty years they have been striving for the goal, accumulating money and knowledge along the way. Retired clients who are worth millions of dollars ask me questions such as "Should I try to get a job to earn enough money to make my IRA contribution this year?" and "Do you really think I can afford to replace this ten-year-old automobile that goes into the shop every other week?"

The common theme for many of my clients, and some of you, is that they have reached the finish line for personal consumption. They have enough money set aside to live on the rest of their lives. If they haven't thought through the numbers, they may not understand it or be aware of it, but within reason, most of the individual decisions for spending or saving are now irrelevant to them and their immediate families.

WHY SET A FINISH LINE?

By "finish line" I am referring, not to the end of life, but to the end of your need to invest in your Family Portfolio (which, remember, includes retirement and college savings). There are three important reasons for identifying the financial finish line in your own life:

1. Setting the finish line makes it real.

Studies show that you have a much higher probability of achieving goals that are specific and formalized in writing. Once you zero in on the bull's-eye, you actually have a chance of hitting it.

2. Finish lines keep you from taking unnecessary risks.

Remember my client from the beginning of chapter 4 who kept the bulk of her assets concentrated in one company's stock because she didn't realize she had crossed the finish line? Unfortunately, hers is not the only example I could give of someone who took extraordinary risks trying to reach a goal he or she had already achieved.

3. Finish lines allow you to redirect assets to more strategic opportunities.

Consider a goal like saving for college. People generally realize when this objective has been accomplished, and then they shift their investment dollars to something else. Why? Because it makes no sense to keep piling up money for a goal that has already been achieved if there are other, more compelling opportunities.

The same can be said of the big finish line: retirement savings. There are a growing number of people who have passed this line and kept saving. For what? Most of the time 50 percent of what's left goes to the government (in estate taxes) and 50 percent to the children. It is good to leave an inheritance for your children, but that goal can be quantified and surpassed as well, and it doesn't compare to eternal investment returns. Once you know and have reached the finish line, you can set your sights firmly on more strategic investment opportunities.

WHAT IS MEANT BY "FINANCIAL INDEPENDENCE"?

Financial independence is that place in time when you have enough. Taking into account pensions, Social Security, and other investments, this is when, by all prudent measures, you no longer need to earn a living. It is oftentimes synonymous with retirement because historically they were one and the same for most people.

Let me be clear that financial independence is not necessarily when you take up golf or tennis as a full-time occupation. It does not always mean you quit working. People today are beginning to realize that some of their most productive years come *after* they stop "making a living" and start "making a life" by doing something they are passionate about. Often this is only possible after many years of financial preparation.

> People today are beginning to realize that some of their most productive years come after they stop "making a living" and start "making a life" by doing something they are passionate about. ∞

For Christians, the term *financial independence* may have some negative connotations because we believe our dependence should always be on God, not on our financial resources. I am in no way saying that you can reach a point where your financial future is secure apart from dependence on God. He ultimately controls the distribution and maintenance of all earthly wealth. However, as part of our faithful management of wealth, there may come a time when we change our overall investment strategy to focus more on our Eternity Portfolio instead of our Family Portfolio. We are instructed to save and prepare for the future and to support our families. However, at some point we may say that enough has been accumulated in the Family Portfolio to last the rest of our lives. This is not an exact science, but it's an effort to determine how much more each of us can put to kingdom uses during our lifetime.

WHAT IF I NEVER GET TO THE FINISH LINE?

Most of us will always have part of our investments going into retirement accounts during our working years. There are lots of people who will never have the perceived security of a sizeable monthly pension or a large investment account. For them, the "finish line" calculations we will run later in this chapter may yield an insurmountable number. What to do then?

There are some obvious steps you can take to reach the finish line, such as extending your working years or cutting back on living expenses. But at the same time, continue investing in your retirement funds *and* continue investing in others through your Eternity Portfolio. We do not know what the future holds, but our heavenly Father does. He knows our needs and He has promised to provide for them. Remember that in any event retirement is still a very short-term goal when compared to eternity.

There are, however, a growing number of people who actually will come to a point where they do not need to add any more to the nest egg. They have crossed the finish line—a good many of them without knowing it. I am convinced that the reason they passed the finish line and kept going is twofold: First, they do not have a vision for the rewards of increasing their ultimate investment, the Eternity Portfolio. In other words, for many people, there *is* nothing better to do with their money, so they continue to accumulate. Second, it is difficult to quantify and understand the finish line for financial independence. Where do you even *start* in trying to calculate a number?

HOW MUCH IS ENOUGH FOR GOOD?

At one time in America, life was simple for those who lived to be retirees. You worked thirty-five to forty years for one company, and that company agreed to pay you a nice pension starting at age sixty-five and lasting the rest of your life. The average life expectancy for people at that time was somewhere in the early seventies, so investing and inflation were not really much of a concern for the five to ten years of an average retirement. More people lived within their means since credit was not nearly as prolific in the culture.

Much has changed in the last twenty years. Today the average employee works at several different companies through the years, few of which even have pension plans. Life expectancies have increased, as have expectations of retired life. Gone are the days of retiring to the rocking chair on the porch. Today, many retirees will spend significantly more money in retirement than they did during their prime working years.

In my observation, there are at least three distinct groups of people preparing for retirement today. The first group is the last wave of the "pensioners." These folks are in their late fifties or sixties and are finishing their long careers at older corporations or government agencies that still provide a meaningful monthly pension benefit. They tend to live within their means, which bodes extremely well for flexibility during their retirement years.

The group at the other end of the spectrum is what I will call the "opportunists," ranging in age from the early twenties to the early forties. None of the opportunists ever seriously believed they would get a pension from a company, and they're probably right. From their earliest working days, the investment mantra has been ringing in their ears, and the smart ones signed up for the maximum 401(k) deferral their first day on the job. They tend to change jobs *as the opportunity presents itself,* and they have understood from day one that whatever they save for retirement is all there is.

The last group is probably in the trickiest position. I'll call them the "transitioners" because they are right in the middle of a monumental change in how retirement is funded. This group tends to be older than forty-five. When the transitioners started their careers, the promise of a pension was still alive and well. Then, in the 1980s and 1990s, just as they were accumulating a few years of service, companies were hit with massive layoffs, restructurings, and pension changes. The result for many of these people is that their standard of living is based on a compensation package (salary and bonus) that is much higher than whatever pension (if any) they will receive in retirement. While many of them have sizeable 401(k) accounts, most of them have no idea how much they need to save to make up the difference over the years of their retirement.

Each of these three groups faces significant challenges when planning for financial independence. First, their income will likely be some combination of pension, Social Security benefits, and investment assets. Second, expenses will vary widely with changes in lifestyle, health, and inflation over the coming years.

With all the variables, how can we possibly come up with a definitive measure of the finish line?

There are all sorts of ways to determine how much money you'll need in retirement. However, keep in mind that this is not an exact science because there are many factors involved. Let's take a look at four factors that will determine how much you will need to fund your retirement.

1. **Cash-Flow Shortfall.** Assume you are retiring today. You expect to draw a pension of $45,000 and Social Security benefits of $11,000 per year, giving you a total annual income of $56,000. (For now, count only "regular" sources of retirement income, not including your investment assets.) After you spend some time reviewing expenses, it becomes obvious that you will need at least $72,000 per year, including taxes, to maintain your current standard of living. Your expenses outweigh your income by $16,000 ($56,000 income minus $72,000 expenses), and that's the amount of your annual shortfall.

   How will you meet this shortfall? Maybe you decide to take on some part-time work. You could always look for places to cut back on expenses, or you could use your accumulated investment assets (which we'll discuss later). In any event, you'll need $16,000 per year to meet the expected shortfall.

   If you do this exercise and have no cash-flow shortfall, you have achieved the finish line of financial independence!

The rest of this discussion is of no consequence to you except to the extent that inflation might catch up with a fixed retirement income.

2. **Life Expectancy.** Once you know your annual shortfall ($16,000 in our earlier example), the next step is determining your life expectancy. How many years will you need to fund the $16,000 shortfall in living expenses? We can only guess at life expectancy, so we should be conservative. (In retirement planning, it is more conservative to plan as if you will live longer.) The average tends to be in the late seventies, but don't plan your retirement based on that. If you are married and you and your spouse are both in reasonable health, there is a pretty good chance that at least one of you will make it into your eighties and maybe even beyond. I would recommend using the number of years until age one hundred to provide a conservative estimate.

3. **Inflation.** Do you ever stop to think how the price of things you buy has increased dramatically over the decades? Consider movie tickets or postage stamps. How many times has the price of these items doubled in the last twenty years? In a similar way, you should expect the cost of living to increase substantially over the period of your retirement. A good guess is probably 3 percent per year for most items and 6 to 10 percent per year for health-related expenses.

4. **Investment Returns.** Those with any experience investing money understand how difficult it is to predict investment returns for one year, much less over a twenty- to thirty-year retirement. Be conservative. Throughout most of the last century, a diversified portfolio consisting entirely of stocks has returned approximately 10 percent per year. But remember, that is not 10 percent year-in and year-out. There are a lot of negative years, such as the ones we saw in the

first part of this decade, that tend to even out the euphoria. My experience is that most people approaching retirement are not comfortable having their entire portfolio in the stock market. If you are not, you must modify your expectation for returns. Why not use a conservative number, say 7 percent, for your investment-return assumption.

How do these four factors come together in helping you set a goal for financial independence? In our example, there is an annual cash shortfall of $16,000. The question is, how much money must I save and invest (at 7 percent annual growth) to be able to withdraw $16,000 per year (adjusted for inflation) for as long as my spouse and I are alive? Whether your annual cash-flow need is $16,000 or $1,000,000 per year, the math is essentially the same.

THE CAPITALIZATION APPROACH

A simple but effective way of getting a general idea of your finish line is called the *capitalization approach*. This method "capitalizes" your cash-flow shortfall into an investment goal. It is a simplified method of taking an annual cash shortfall and determining a rough estimate of how much you will need to set aside for your entire retirement. Once you have accumulated investment assets equal to the capitalized goal, you know that you have achieved your finish line.

Use the worksheet on page 82 to make a rough calculation of your personal financial-independence finish line. Our example is based on a conservative capitalization rate of 25 times your cash-flow shortfall. Although it may sound simplistic, there is a great degree of complexity woven into the magical "25 times" capitalization rate. Where does this come from?

Let's say a sixty-year-old woman needs $16,000 per year for every year of her retirement. If we assess her life expectancy at one hundred, she will need assets to cover forty years of retirement. Forty times $16,000 equals $640,000. However, because her invested assets will grow over the forty years, she doesn't really need as much as $640,000 right now. On the other hand, because of inflation, the cost of living will increase every year and she will need more than $16,000 annually. Given all these variables, how do we determine the right "finish line"?

As a conservative rule of thumb, some financial advisors like to plan for an individual to withdraw no more than 4 percent of his or her retirement assets annually. Why 4 percent? Because if we estimate that the investments grow at 7 percent annually (based on the historical averages for a diversified portfolio), the return should offset inflation and the withdrawal, while continuing to grow modestly. We can't count on that 7 percent return every year, as there will be good years and bad. However, based on history and a properly diversified portfolio, there is almost no probability of an individual running out of money with a 4 percent withdrawal rate.

So if 4 percent is our target withdrawal rate, we can determine how much is needed in savings for any amount of annual shortfall by multiplying the shortfall by 25 (the inverse of 4 percent).

In our example, to get our capitalized goal we would multiply our $16,000 shortfall by 25, giving us a finish line of $400,000. Now what exactly does that mean? The $400,000 represents a conservative estimate of what you would want to have invested in retirement savings in order to draw 4 percent annually ($16,000 in the first year) for the remainder of your lifetime. Because you are using a percentage, the actual withdrawal would be adjusted each year; in other words, as the account grows over time, your withdrawal grows as well to keep up with inflation.

Four hundred thousand dollars may sound like a huge number to yield only $16,000 per year in cash flow. In some ways that is true. For example, if you calculated an exact finish line based on achieving 7 percent returns *every year* for exactly thirty years, the investment needed would be more like $290,000. The problem with this smaller goal is that it is much more likely to be used up prematurely given the variability of investment returns, the uncertainty about life expectancy, and the rising cost of living.

In other words, if everything works out exactly as planned, you can get by on less. Just be prepared for the possibility of having to de-

CAPITALIZATION APPROACH

Investment assets needed for financial independence

INCOME IN RETIREMENT

Pension	_____	
Social Security	_____	
Part-time work	_____	
_____	_____	
TOTAL INCOME	_____	**A**

LIVING EXPENSES IN RETIREMENT

Housing	_____	
Food	_____	
Medical	_____	
Insurance	_____	
Taxes	_____	
Recreation	_____	
Gifts	_____	
Clothing	_____	
Utilities	_____	
_____	_____	
TOTAL EXPENSES	_____	**B**

INVESTMENTS IN RETIREMENT

Eternity Portfolio Investments	_____	**C**

NET CASH FLOW IN RETIREMENT | _____ | **D**

(A – B – C)

If **D** is negative, multiply by -25 | _____ | **E**

crease your expenses if the money runs out. On the other hand, the $400,000 will likely provide some inheritance for your children or a bequest to charity upon your death. Obviously if you start with an assumption that your investments will earn substantially more than 7 percent over time, you will be able to withdraw more (or save less) to accomplish the same purpose.

Understand that your financial-independence finish line is only an estimate. It is useful to determine whether or not you are on the right track with your retirement savings. For some of you, this will be a wake-up call to invest in retirement. For others, however, this calculation will show that you have no cash shortfall—in fact, that you long ago passed the finish line. That is when you must give serious thought to the more strategic investment opportunities of the Eternity Portfolio.

WHAT HAPPENS AFTER I CROSS THE FINISH LINE?

Rick and Barbara Cohen (see Case Study 5, page 177) have been praying for some time about their Eternity Portfolio. In recent years their assets have increased significantly, especially the stock options in Rick's company. Barbara is the founding partner of a small CPA (certified public accounting) firm in San Francisco, where they live, and her business has prospered as well. By all reasonable calculations, Rick and Barbara have more than they will need to support their family going forward.

After much deliberation, the Cohens have decided to exercise and sell a large portion of Rick's stock options and invest $1.7 million in their Eternity Portfolio. Part of that amount will be placed in a Donor-Advised Fund to be distributed over the coming years, primarily to strategic ministries to the homeless in San Francisco. They intend to invest $2 million in a Charitable Remainder Trust. (We'll talk more about these techniques in chapter 8.) Finally, Rick and Barbara will make additional investments in the years ahead when more of Rick's stock options are exercised and Barbara's CPA firm is sold at retirement.

Note that many people have reached financial independence without a large amount of assets. Case Study 4 (page 174) gives the example of Ben Richards, who makes $28,000 per year. Ben is a fifty-seven-year-old widower whose children are almost grown. As he looks toward retirement, Ben expects his pension and Social Security benefits to exceed his living expenses. Having accumulated some modest investment assets, Ben decides that he can begin to invest excess cash exclusively in his Eternity Portfolio.

One last example of "How much is enough for good?" is the Fleming family (Case Study 3, page 171). Todd and Emily Fleming are in their early forties and have four children, ages eight to fourteen. Todd recently sold his first company, Industrial Solutions, for $30 million. Although he has been told by some well-meaning friends that he should consider retiring to work in some sort of full-time Christian ministry, Todd feels that God really wants him to start a new business. He and Emily believe God has specially equipped Todd to be an entrepreneur and fund ministries by way of the revenues generated from his business. They plan to invest $23 million of the sale proceeds in a new business venture. Next, the Flemings plan to donate $3 million to several strategic ministries, including their church. Finally, the Fleming Family Foundation will be established and funded with $2 million to be used for making later gifts. Emily is also considering the idea of establishing a crisis-pregnancy clinic with funds from the foundation. (We'll discuss more on foundations in chapter 8.)

ADDITIONAL OBSERVATIONS

You may be saying to yourself, "That's great for people who have a lot of money or a nice pension, but what about me? I've been saving for retirement for years but will never have 'enough' based on these definitions." First, take heart; there are lots of people in your same situation and many more who are worse off. The important thing is to continue to invest in your Eternity Portfolio even while you have the financial-independence finish line in front of you.

It is true that for most people, financial independence will not happen by age fifty-five—and maybe not by sixty-five, either. Is that a bad thing? God created us for work, *even if we don't need the money!* Since many jobs no longer require the physical exertion they once did, we are blessed to live in a period where we can continue to be productive well past the historical retirement age.

I've heard countless stories of people who retired from their jobs and then "retired" from this life shortly thereafter. Their purpose for living was inextricably connected to their employment. To avoid this, make sure you find something you enjoy doing, something you are passionate about. This will provide a purpose even if (maybe *especially* if) you have achieved financial independence.

Remember, your identity is not ultimately wrapped up in how much money you make or what your occupation is, but instead in the fact that you are a child of God. Retirement and financial independence can be wonderful benefits to some Christians, who suddenly have more time for service than ever before. If you find yourself in this category, consider volunteering in a ministry you feel passionate about—whether it's the children's club at your church, a homeless shelter in town, a tutoring program at your local high school, or an upcoming citywide evangelistic outreach.

> ∞
>
> *Financial independence is merely the opportunity to put your eternal investments into high gear.*

This point is key: Your investment in the Eternity Portfolio should not be put on hold until you reach the finish line of financial independence. In chapter 4 the discussion focused on making this most-critical investment while at the same time allocating resources to other shorter-term goals, such as retirement. *Financial independence is merely the opportunity to put your eternal investments into high gear.* It is the chance to finish strong, to make some extraordinary investments in the latter part of your life. But don't wait. Remember the story of the rich fool in the Bible. He thought he could continue saving for himself, but he didn't realize he had no control over his future (Luke 12:15-21).

Make sure you are making eternal investments throughout the journey of life so that whenever it does end, you will have made the most of your opportunities.

CHAPTER 5
Funding the Portfolio Part 2: How Much Is Enough for Good?

DISCUSSION QUESTIONS

1. What does retirement mean to you? Financial independence? Relaxation? Moving from full-time to part-time work? An opportunity for ministry?

2. Have you established a financial finish line for your life savings? If so, how has that impacted your outlook on life? work? money?

3. Is financial independence a worthy goal for a Christian? Why or why not?

4. Should your life be different once you reach "financial independence"? If so, how?

5. If you have already reached the point where financially it appears that you have "enough," what are you doing with the excess? Might God be leading you to invest significantly more in your Eternity Portfolio right now?

6. If retirement and financial independence seem out of reach for you, what should your response be?

CHAPTER 6
God's Asset Allocation

In This Chapter:

■ God's plan for your "giving" investments
■ Where to invest
■ What types of investments to make
■ How to design your Eternity Portfolio focused
  on your personal mission

Once you really get motivated to start investing, say for retirement, where do you start? Did you know that there are literally hundreds of thousands of investments available in the market? Which types will best meet your needs?

Investing strategy begins with funding and then progresses to portfolio design. Although there is certainly room for spontaneous investments, the foundation for a successful portfolio is laid with a well-designed strategy.

When a new client comes to my office, we first engage in extensive planning. Then I normally spend two to three hours talking with him or her about the broad landscape of investments before giving specific recommendations. For example, we'll talk about "asset allocation," which is the process of deciding which of the major investment "asset classes"—broad categories of investments such as cash, bonds, stocks, real estate, and commodities (gold, for example)—should be included in the portfolio and to what extent. Only after the portfolio is designed and the different investment categories are identified can the actual

investments be made. At that point, specific stocks and bonds are purchased.

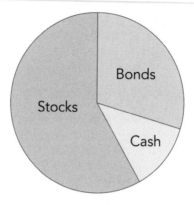

I believe that in order to make informed decisions, you must have
some understanding of the context of your investments. Studies have
shown that the effectiveness of an investment portfolio over time is
largely determined by design. Having an accurate perspective on the
overall investing universe is just as important as selecting the actual
investments.

This principle applies to the Eternity Portfolio as well. This chapter
is meant to give you the "lay of the land" when it comes to the major
design considerations for your Eternity Portfolio. The decision of *how
much* to invest is only the first step. Andrew Carnegie summed it up
best when he described the difficulty of giving away wealth in a strategic manner:

> It is well to remember that it requires the exercise of not less ability
> than that which acquires it, to use wealth so as to be really
> beneficial to the community.[13]

As you focus on giving as investing, you quickly realize that the
questions of *where, what,* and *how* are the most difficult ongoing decisions for the faithful manager. Fortunately we are not left to figure
these out for ourselves. God has clearly described His priorities (or as-

set classes) for our giving. To be most effective, our eternal investments must be aligned with His overarching purpose. It's not coincidence that these are the same priorities He has for the other parts of our lives.

Let's start with the big picture—which can't get any bigger than the greatest commandments mentioned by Jesus:

> Then one of them, a lawyer, asked Him a question, testing Him, and saying, "Teacher, which is the great commandment in the law?"
>
> Jesus said to him, "'You shall love the Lord your God with all your heart, with all your soul, and with all your mind.' This is the first and great commandment. And the second is like it: 'You shall love your neighbor as yourself.'" (Matthew 22:35-39)

In these brief words Jesus summarized thousands of years of laws and prophetic commands. *Love God first; then love people.* Jesus also gave us the great commission, which gets a little more specific. This is what should be the primary long-term objective of all Christian activity:

> Go therefore and make disciples of all the nations, baptizing them in the name of the Father and of the Son and of the Holy Spirit, teaching them to observe all things that I have commanded you; and lo, I am with you always, even to the end of the age. (Matthew 28:19-20)

It's clear that these commands of Jesus should affect the way we live. But they should also affect the way we give! As Christians, we should build our Eternity Portfolio to carry out the great commandments and fund the great commission. The resources God has provided over and above our needs should be invested to share the love of Christ with others.

This chapter will help you understand the investing universe from God's perspective. It is only as you understand the "big picture" Christian mission that you can identify your part within it and design your Eternity Portfolio accordingly.

We will go through a process that should enable you to build your portfolio design in some detail. Your portfolio will be as individual as everything else about you. If you are married, you and your spouse both need to give input, and you should reach a mutually agreeable solution. For families with children, the Eternity Portfolio is a great starting place to widen their vision for God's kingdom. Each family member can have a part.

As you begin to design your portfolio, ask yourself the following questions:

1. Where should I be making an impact with my giving?
2. What am I trying to accomplish with my giving?
3. How has God specifically gifted and called me to achieve these goals?

WHERE?

JERUSALEM, JUDEA, AND THE WORLD

God's plan has always been for the whole world. "For God so loved the *world* that He gave His only begotten Son, that whoever believes in Him should not perish but have everlasting life" (John 3:16, emphasis added). Over the last two thousand years the Good News of Jesus Christ has radiated outward from a small area in the Middle East to most of the known world. This was no accident. Before His ascension to heaven Jesus left the disciples further instructions about the great commission. He knew that without specific guidance, they might feel that their sole responsibility was the nation of Israel. Jesus made it clear that His plan was much bigger than that:

> But you shall receive power when the Holy Spirit has come upon you; and you shall be witnesses to Me in Jerusalem, and in all Judea and Samaria, and to the end of the earth. (Acts 1:8)

The disciples were to impact their local area (Jerusalem), their region (Judea and Samaria), and the whole globe ("the end of the earth"). We are entrusted with the same mission today. God is working around the world, and we want to be a part of it. Therefore, the first level of decision we should make with our Eternity Portfolio is where our investments will be focused.

Note that many charitable organizations are making a significant impact in more than one area of the world. Some churches are a prime example. My church has a major emphasis in all three areas and is making a difference on these fronts simultaneously. Examples include our benevolence ministry to the poor (local), leadership training conferences (regional), and strategic church-planting efforts (global). It can be helpful to attempt to categorize your investments based on their *focus*.

Local. Most people invest the largest part of their giving locally. Programs that benefit local churches, schools, hospitals, and so forth are popular for obvious reasons: People see the benefit of their giving on a regular basis. Results are easier to measure. Loyalty and a sense of community are also major factors.

In this setting, we are defining "local" as local to the donor. An example of a local investment is a community homeless shelter. Although the indirect benefits of the organization can certainly reach other areas, the primary focus is meeting the needs of the local population.

In addition to the reasons listed above, you will probably want to have a significant part of your portfolio focused locally because of the witness this represents in the community. It has been said that "the light that shines farthest shines brightest at home." Our platform for personal witness often begins with our investments close to home.

Regional. Regional investments extend our view beyond community to the outer reaches of our cultural boundaries. An organization ministering across the United States would be an example. Also included in this category would be a ministry focused on a particular area, need, or people group (e.g., Native Americans) here in the United States.

The advantage of the regional category is obviously that more people are directly impacted by the organization than with a local ministry. In the normal growth process of a successful ministry there is a natural tendency to expand coverage area. This can bring a whole set of new challenges as the organization grows, however, and must be done with care.

Global. Global investments are focused outside our cultural boundaries. They might also work within our region or local area, but the main thrust is elsewhere around the world. An example might be a relief organization that works all over the world to reduce poverty and hunger.

Compared to local or even regional investments, there are significant advantages and disadvantages, from the investor's perspective, to global organizations. One major advantage is the lower cost of living in many countries as compared to the United States. Money just goes farther. Another advantage is that the "harvest" can be much higher if God is really moving in one country versus another. For example, in the last twenty years, Christianity has swept across countries like South Korea and even underground in China while experiencing a decline or very little growth in Europe. The major disadvantage is that the long-distance nature of the projects makes accountability much more difficult.

WHAT?

REACHING, TEACHING, AND MINISTERING TO NEEDS

We have been instructed to go into all the world and make disciples. Along the way we are to share Christ's love by loving our neighbors as ourselves. My church has broken out this mission into three broad tasks:

1. Reaching people with the gospel of Christ (evangelism),
2. Teaching Christians biblical truth about how to live as disciples of Christ (discipleship), and

3. Ministering to physical, emotional, and spiritual needs in the name of Christ (mercy).

These three categories are straight out of the great commandments and great commission. All of the investments we make in the Eternity Portfolio fall into these three broad "asset classes." Let's look at each class in more detail.

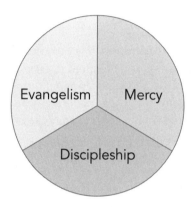

GOD'S ASSET ALLOCATION

Evangelism

Throughout history the prophets, evangelists, and preachers of God have been funded by faithful men and women. From Elijah (1 Kings 17) to the disciples (Luke 9), God has used His people to invest in the spread of the gospel. Jesus spoke about the importance of supporting this effort:

> *He who receives you receives Me, and he who receives Me receives Him who sent Me. He who receives a prophet in the name of a prophet shall receive a prophet's reward. And he who receives a righteous man in the name of a righteous man shall receive a righteous man's reward. And whoever gives one of these little ones only a cup of cold water in the name of a disciple, assuredly, I say to you, he shall by no means lose his reward.* (Matthew 10:40-42)

You can be involved in funding evangelism in many different ways. These range from the obvious—such as giving to a citywide outreach event—to the not-so-obvious—such as investing in a ministry that translates Scripture into different languages.

Many organizations within the Christian community have evangelistic motives. However, when building your portfolio, keep in mind we are looking at the *focus* of the ministry as a differentiator.

The major sectors within evangelistic organizations include Bible translation/distribution, church planting, and group/event focus. There can be additional categories within each of these.

Bible translation/distribution is a straightforward category describing those organizations committed to making the Word of God available to all people in all languages around the world.

Church planting includes organizations as well as individuals who develop strategies and train pastors to start Christian communities in traditional and nontraditional settings. In some countries these churches are simply groups of believers meeting in each other's houses. Many missionaries are part of the church-planting category.

Finally, **group/event** focus tends to be the "large numbers" strategies such as crusades, festivals, and other gatherings intended to expose many people at a time to the message of Jesus Christ. Also within this category would be organizations that use a specific activity as an opportunity to reach out within the community while offering an important service. Sports camps and school campus programs would be examples of this type of organization.

EVANGELISM		
Church planting	Bible translation and distribution	Group/event focus

Explore the different opportunities and learn where God is working. You may be surprised at the sheer magnitude of what is going on in every facet of life. For example, in the athletics arena, a program called Upward Basketball began as a way to help local children through organized sports. An athletic league that is open to the public, Upward Basketball holds practices and games at the church sponsoring the program. At each event there is a break in the activity, and one of the participants shares a testimony about what God has done in his or her life. As this program has spread through churches around the country, it has expanded to include cheerleading, soccer, and other sports. Investing in Upward Basketball is a way to share the Good News of Jesus Christ.

> We have been instructed to go into all the world and make disciples. Along the way we are to share Christ's love by loving our neighbors as ourselves.
>
> ∞

On a completely different front, some of the most strategic activity in the world today is going on behind the scenes through a strategy called "saturation church planting." As opposed to a missionary, say from America, going to start a church in a foreign country, U.S.–based organizations form strategic alliances with groups of believers in that country. Local leaders who are called to be pastors are discipled and trained to be church planters and given the vision of teaching those skills to others. Often the trainers and training materials are funded by partnerships in the U.S. In this way church planting *movements* have been birthed and have experienced exponential (as opposed to additive) growth across whole regions. Investing in church planting is evangelism.

It's almost impossible to overestimate the impact of Christians investing selflessly in this area. Listen to the following account:

> The history of the first two centuries of Christianity abounds with remarkable facts, showing with what zeal and entireness of soul, the church went into the work of converting the world. Those who periled their lives and suffered the loss of all things in preaching, were not the only ones who made sacrifices for the spread of the

gospel. Some spent all besides a bare support of themselves, to furnish the means of evangelizing others; those who had no property gave the avails of their labor; and it is recorded of one man that he sold himself as a slave to a heathen family, to get access to them for their conversion, and for years cheerfully endured the labor and condition of a slave till he succeeded with the whole family, and took his liberty from the gratitude of the converts. . . . The fires of such benevolence, burning wherever a company of Christians was gathered, could not fail soon to overspread the world, and in the space of one generation most of the nations then known to the civilized world, were more or less evangelized. And if such a tone of benevolent action could be now restored to the church, another generation would not pass before the earth would be 'full of the knowledge and glory of God, as the waters cover the sea.'[14]

Discipleship

The second major asset class within the Eternity Portfolio is discipleship—the opportunity to invest in people and organizations that are focused on the spiritual growth of the church. The apostle Paul spent much of his time teaching new converts how to be fully devoted followers of Jesus Christ. Paul generated much of his own support through his secular trade of tent making, but he gave clear, common-sense guidance in this area: "Let him who is taught the word share in all good things with him who teaches" (Galatians 6:6). Elsewhere when speaking of teachers, Jesus states that "the laborer is worthy of his wages" (Luke 10:7).

Within the Christian community today there are many different types of organizations aimed at discipleship. The major categories include counseling, Christian education, and research or curriculum development.

Counseling ministries focus on the one-on-one interaction that can take place over a variety of topics including marriage, finances, and spiritual growth. The purpose is to help Christians (and often non-

Christians) overcome obstacles in their lives and serve God more fully.

Christian education is typically broad-based group discipleship. Radio programs, Bible studies, Christian schools and universities—all these and more fall into this category.

The last category, **research and curriculum development,** is composed of organizations primarily focused on developing discipleship tools (such as apologetics or small-group studies). Other organizations address political, scientific, or medical issues from a Christian worldview.

DISCIPLESHIP		
Counseling	Christian education	Research/curriculum development

Mercy

Ministering to the needs of the poor receives more explicit emphasis in the Bible than any other area of giving. Verse after verse encourages those who love God to engage in this tangible expression of His love for others. Let's look at just a few of the many verses:

> If there is among you a poor man of your brethren, within any of the gates in your land which the Lord your God is giving you, you shall not harden your heart nor shut your hand from your poor brother. (Deuteronomy 15:7)

> Blessed is he who considers the poor; the Lord will deliver him in time of trouble. The Lord will preserve him and keep him alive, and he will be blessed on the earth. (Psalm 41:1-2)

> He who has pity on the poor lends to the Lord, and He will pay back what he has given. (Proverbs 19:17)

> *He who has a generous eye will be blessed, for he gives of his*
> *bread to the poor.* (Proverbs 22:9)

It was obvious from His teaching and actions that Jesus was passionate about the plight of the poor, the sick, and the helpless. He fed them, healed them, and gave them hope regularly during His earthly ministry. When He counseled the rich young ruler, Jesus indicated that giving to the poor would result in treasure in heaven for those who followed Him:

> *Jesus said to him, "If you want to be perfect, go, sell what you*
> *have and give to the poor, and you will have treasure in heaven;*
> *and come, follow Me."* (Matthew 19:21)

As the love of Christ is lived out in our lives, a natural result is that we love helping people, especially those who can't help themselves. We can also see this emphasis in the early church. An organized task force was established for collecting and administering gifts to the poor (Acts 4:32-37; 6:1-7). And Paul was continuously taking up money for the poor as he traveled from church to church (Romans 15:25-27, 2 Corinthians 8–9).

The mercy category can be divided into three main areas. The first resides at the most basic level of human need: **food/clothing/shelter.** In addition to obvious investments such as homeless shelters and food pantries, this includes humanitarian relief organizations in war-torn and poverty-stricken regions around the world.

Another subcategory is **health care,** which covers research, treatment, and preventive measures. Free or discounted health clinics, humanitarian medical care in foreign countries, hospice care centers—all are examples of this category.

And then there is **life-skills training,** which focuses on training, literacy, and microenterprise as the means to break the poverty cycle. For example, there are organizations and some churches that provide training such as ESL (English as a second language) and computer skills. Microenterprise is a relatively new concept in the international community whereby small loans—maybe just $100—are made to individuals who use the funds to start a business making textiles or farming.

MERCY		
Food/shelter/ clothing	Health care	Life skills training

There are two main reasons you want to be invested in the mercy category. First, helping those who cannot help themselves is an outward display of the love of God in your heart. John wrote of this to the early Christians:

> By this we know love, because He laid down His life for us. And we also ought to lay down our lives for the brethren. But whoever has this world's goods, and sees his brother in need, and shuts up his heart from him, how does the love of God abide in him? (1 John 3:16-17)

James, the brother of Jesus, carries this theme in his writing as well:

> Pure and undefiled religion before God and the Father is this: to visit orphans and widows in their trouble. (James 1:27)

Caring for the poor has been a hallmark of Christian love from the very beginning. Reports such as the following were common:

> And their kindness to the poor was boundless. Christians felt as much bound to this as to prayer, or to the hearing of the gospel. Contributions and actual exertions for their relief were made indispensable parts of Sabbath exercises. At the close of public worship, lists of the needy, the widows and orphans, were produced and considered, and additions were made from time to

time as new cases occurred; and the wants of these were supplied from the funds gathered by free contributions. No heart-stirring appeals were needed to awake dormant sympathies.[15]

As Christ has loved us and given Himself for us, we are to do likewise for the hurting and helpless.

Second, the mercy sector is in many ways the *facilitator* of the other parts of the Christian mission. Physical needs take precedence over spiritual needs. If a person is starving, he likely won't be able to consider spiritual issues until his hunger is satisfied.

For example, my business partner Dave Polstra coordinates a medical partnership between several U.S. churches and a church in Guatemala. Teams of doctors, dentists, and assistants from the U.S. make trips to Guatemala to provide medical services to people in the mountain villages of that area. As part of their visit to the clinic, the local people have the opportunity to hear about Jesus and understand the love that compels these volunteers to share of their time, skills, and money.

Blended Investments

Many organizations are focused in more than one major area. From a practical *and* theological sense, it is often difficult to tell where mercy ends and evangelism begins, or where evangelism ends and discipleship begins. In fact, the best organizations will have elements of each. There is no need to make rigid distinctions when building your portfolio. However, I have found it helpful when evaluating investments to identify the *major thrust* of each organization for purposes of the portfolio.

HOW?

YOUR UNIQUE OPPORTUNITIES

Hugh O. Maclellan, Jr., is president of the Maclellan Foundation, a large Christian grant-making foundation in Chattanooga, Tennessee.

As one in a long family line of faithful managers, he has spent years refining the giving strategy of his own family as well as that of the Maclellan Foundation. In his testimony Hugh talks about the way he and his wife have built their Eternity Portfolio, which starts at 70 percent of their income. First, 10 percent of their income is allocated to their local church. Then 15 percent goes to what they call "small sustaining" gifts. These include helping needy families as the opportunities arise, "dollar swapping" (you support my favorite charity, I'll support yours), and other gifts of encouragement that arise spontaneously. The final and largest area of the Maclellan's personal giving is 45 percent to what they consider strategic investments. Their two major focuses in their strategic category are evangelism and mercy.

By now you have gotten a sense for the Eternity Portfolio investing universe, and we can now look at how those fit into your particular portfolio. Even though you may not be investing 70 percent of your income, you can still be just as strategic with how you allocate your giving. It takes time and intentional focus, but as you design your portfolio, there are some parameters you will want to consider. Start with a framework something like this:

DESIGNING MY ETERNITY PORTFOLIO

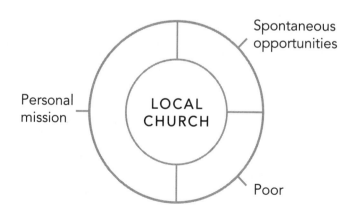

THE LOCAL CHURCH—A CORE INVESTMENT

When designing the stock portion of a traditional investment portfolio, the first thing we install is a core holding of large U.S. company stocks. The purpose of this core holding is to provide solid long-term returns in an area of the market (large multinational corporations) that has been well-defined and evaluated over many decades. For some people with limited resources, this may be their entire portfolio strategy. Those who have larger portfolios take advantage of other more focused investments (those with higher risk/return potential) in addition to the core holding.

In much the same way, systematic giving to your local church can be seen as a core investment in your Eternity Portfolio. Strategic, discipling churches that are committed to the Holy Scriptures and fulfilling the great commission make a powerful difference for the kingdom of God. Let me share six key reasons why your Eternity Portfolio should start with at least a 10 percent investment in your church.

1. **Informed, coordinated effort.** The church is uniquely positioned to be aware of needs in the local community and to guide the activity of its members to effective ministry. The book of Acts tells how the early church members brought their gifts to the leaders, who organized and directed their use (see Acts 4, 6).

2. **Diversification.** Strategic churches have paid staff and volunteers who, working as a team, are able to focus simultaneously on specific elements of the threefold mission: evangelism, discipleship, and mercy. Nowhere else will you find this immediate coverage of all "asset classes" in your portfolio.

3. **Worship.** Giving is supremely an act of worship. Just as you regularly focus on prayer, praise, and preaching during church services, the giving process is a vital part of worship.

4. **Personal benefit.** I am frequently amazed at the way many Christians enjoy the benefits of church programs, facilities,

and support without ever feeling compelled to help fund them. Invest in the organizations that are investing in the spiritual, social, and physical development of you and your family.

5. **Personal opportunity.** The church presents your best opportunity to be involved *with* your investment. In addition to your money, you can invest freely of your time and abilities. Your church offers on-the-job training and involvement in almost every sphere of ministry.

6. **Accountability.** Few organizations have as much transparency to the donor as the local church. Typically within the church you have welcome access to the senior pastor, key department directors, and the annual budget. You are able to see firsthand the results of your investment.

PERSONAL MISSION—FOCUS ON YOUR CALLING

The mission of the church is quite broad. However, God has equipped each member to be most effective in his or her area of special calling.

> Now you are the body of Christ, and members individually. And God has appointed these in the church: first apostles, second prophets, third teachers, after that miracles, then gifts of healings, helps, administrations, varieties of tongues. Are all apostles? Are all prophets? Are all teachers? (1 Corinthians 12:27-29)

In this passage Paul is saying that we have each been uniquely gifted and motivated. You need to determine where your calling lies and pursue that with your time, abilities, and investments. In our example above, one of Hugh Maclellan's passions is evangelism and, in particular, church planting. The strategic section of his Eternity Portfolio is invested in his calling. In my case, it is discipleship (specifically in the areas of faithful life management and leadership training). The most strategic investments I have are in that area. Not only do I focus my money there, I also spend much of my time doing those activities.

A significant portion of your "nonchurch" investing should be focused on your God-given calling in ministry. It is also quite possible that some of your most strategic opportunities will arise within your local church. From a portfolio-management standpoint, I would classify those investments under your personal mission.

Perhaps you have no idea about what personal mission God has called you to. That's okay, but start searching now. Begin praying for God to specifically lead you to His plan. Study the Bible for insight. You may find yourself being drawn to a broad area, such as evangelism, and then gradually realize your gifts fit with something more specific within that area, such as being a counselor at a citywide outreach festival. Or your sense of God's calling may come the other way around: first you sense that God has laid on your heart a passion for helping women in crisis pregnancies, and later you begin to understand how that fits in the broader area of mercy.

> ∞ | *The intersection of your personal mission with your giving is one of the most powerful combinations you can ever experience.*

There are tools that can help you evaluate your areas of giftedness. Organizations such as Halftime (www.halftime.org) have some great resources to help you plan out your personal life strategy to the glory of God. Generous Giving offers an on-line profiling tool (www.GenerousGiving.org) that will lead you through questions regarding your calling in the areas of evangelism, discipleship, and mercy. Seek God's will in prayer and Bible study. You will know when you find it because your energy and passion for life and ministry will explode.

As God leads, invest your money. The intersection of your personal mission with your giving is one of the most powerful combinations you can ever experience. True joy and fulfillment in Christ are the result of having your life in alignment with God's purpose. Your effectiveness for the kingdom of God will multiply exponentially as you move in this direction.

REMEMBER THE POOR

Based on the overwhelming coverage of the topic in Scripture, I can only conclude that God *really* wants us to give to the poor. In no other specific area of giving do we see such repeated promises of blessing for obedience and warning for failure. God wants us to take the time and invest resources to help those who cannot help themselves and who will not be able to reciprocate. I cannot help but think that a major part of God's plan to reveal Himself to the world is through the righteous and selfless acts of Christians. We need to get in on this plan.

Unfortunately, waste and corruption have often been the hallmark of government welfare programs. This is a grave concern to us as strategic investors since we have no interest in funding programs that perpetuate the poverty cycle or giving money that gets siphoned off to special-interest groups. However, our responsibility to remember the poor is not lessened by the potential for abuse. There *are* organizations that operate effectively in this sector. If you take the time to understand the organizations you support, you can lessen the likelihood that your investment will be wasted or mismanaged. (We'll talk more about this concept in chapter 7.) When it comes to gifts to help struggling families or individuals, we should try to have discernment but err on the side of generosity. There is no telling how God will use your gifts to make a difference for someone else.

My wife, Melissa, was recently concerned about a family in our church that she knew was having a difficult time financially. As we discussed how God might want us to be involved in helping, Melissa decided to call some mutual friends to see if they wanted to participate in the joy of what was to be an anonymous "investment pool." The response was overwhelming. In just a matter of days she collected a sizable gift from about ten families. When Melissa passed along the money to the family, she said simply that the funds had been "given to us to give to them." That is how God planned it. He gives us money, some of which is meant for others. The response from this grateful family was praise to God for how He had answered their prayers through an unknown source. They said that in the past God had blessed them to be able to give to others, and now they were on the receiving end.

SPONTANEOUS GIVING—READY FOR THE UNEXPECTED

Spontaneous giving brings joy. Sometimes the opportunity is a missionary in a developing country who needs a new power generator. Maybe a family just lost their home in a flood. It could be a new, radical discipling strategy or a matching-grant opportunity.

Whatever the cause, most of us are wired to respond to urgent cries for help. The problem arises when we must look around for available funds to meet that need—which typically means unplanned personal sacrifice. Now you have a doubly complicated decision—*Should I help with this present situation, and if so, where do I cut back personally to free up the cash?*

My recommendation is that you allocate some funds in your Eternity Portfolio to a "Spontaneous" or "Other" category that would be available for unanticipated giving opportunities. This concept has made all the difference in the joy Melissa and I feel in giving. Because we have set aside funds specifically for the purpose of investing in new ways, we are actively looking for where God would have us direct that money.

There will also be times when you are led to make some truly sacrificial, unplanned investments. Faith is really tested as you decide whether to follow God's leading or ignore it. Don't miss the blessing just because it seems to be outside of your systematic strategy. There is an indescribable joy that comes from seeing God work in unusual ways through you. Of course, the wisdom to know whether a particular opportunity is from God comes only after much time spent in communion with Him.

BRINGING IT ALL TOGETHER

The chart on the next page shows the four stages of developing one's Eternity Portfolio: the three eternal asset classes; subsectors of those asset classes; categories of your own unique opportunities and mission; and finally specific investments.

MY ETERNITY PORTFOLIO

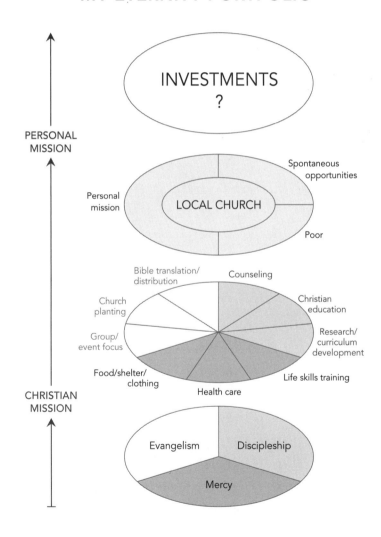

Once you have mapped out your portfolio design, it's time to begin the implementation and choose your specific investments. In the next chapter we'll look at approaches that will help you make wise, strategic decisions for your Eternity Portfolio.

CHAPTER 6
God's Asset Allocation

DISCUSSION QUESTIONS

1. How might thinking about your giving in terms of a portfolio of investments change your perspective?

2. What do you think about the idea that God has given instructions in the Bible for maximizing your Eternity Portfolio? Do you agree with the three "asset classes" of evangelism, discipleship, and mercy? If not, what do you think is missing?

3. In the past, how have you thought about giving to the poor? How has God molded your views in this area? Based on what you read in Scripture, should your current giving have a greater or lesser emphasis on the poor?

4. If you have not supported your local church in the past, why not? Did any of the six reasons on pages 104–105 convince you to begin? If you have faithfully supported your local church, how has that impacted you? What results have you seen?

5. Have you ever thought about your personal mission? After reading the information in this chapter, in what areas do you believe God would have you focus your giving?

6. How can you be more sensitive to God's leading as it relates to spontaneous giving opportunities? Does your Eternity Portfolio currently include a category for this so that money is available when needed?

Remember to visit www.EternityPortfolio.com to continue the practical work of setting up your Eternity Portfolio on-line.

CHAPTER 7

Making Wise Investments

In This Chapter:

- ■ Accountability and your Eternity Portfolio
- ■ What to look for in a good investment
- ■ Asking the right questions
- ■ The Eternity Portfolio investment policy statement

Think about your retirement portfolio for a moment. How did you choose your investments? For example, once you made the decision to invest in stocks, how did you select them? Did you receive a phone call from the CEO of a new company and decide on the spot to invest your hard-earned money in his venture? Maybe you scanned the list of publicly traded stocks in *The Wall Street Journal* and selected a handful of noteworthy companies. How about this—an acquaintance e-mailed you about a startup company with a great idea for reaching a vast, untapped market. She had just invested some money in the company and thought it would be a great opportunity for you as well.

Any of this sound familiar? The irony is that these scenarios could describe either the typical investing process *or* the giving process of many individuals, especially in recent years. Unfortunately, most people who invested this way incurred devastating losses in the stock market in 2000 and 2001. Poor management, lack of vision, naïveté, overpromotion, and in some cases outright fraud served to deprive investors of the long-term gains they hoped to achieve.

Sadly, *every year* much of what people believe to be invested for eternity is lost in the exact same way. And many donors neither realize nor care that this is happening.

STRIVING FOR ACCOUNTABILITY

Although we may receive an annual report from the organizations we support, it is often woefully lacking in the sort of performance data we demand from our traditional investments. Once a gift is made, we assume our responsibility in the process has ended—or, more likely, we simply forget about it. This is exacerbated by the fact that most charities have little incentive to report how funds have been used until they approach you for the next "investment"—and then only if the results were favorable. (However, some organizations are very good at keeping donors updated; not surprisingly, these strategic ministries receive more funding and tend to be more effective over the long term.)

Another reason most people "never look back" when it comes to giving is that they themselves do not feel *accountable* for their giving decisions. After all, it's not the same as your retirement portfolio where a poor decision can set back your retirement date a few years. Or is it? Until you develop a true understanding of eternal rewards, your gifts will have no long-term significance to you personally.

Accountability is the key. Whether managing a traditional investment portfolio or the Eternity Portfolio, faithful managers are accountable and *require* this virtue in their investments.

Accountability for the investor involves taking steps to be certain that investments are researched, evaluated, and monitored to achieve the best long-term results for the portfolio. This includes holding the investments (organizations) accountable for achieving their stated objectives efficiently and on a timely basis. For Christian organizations, we would add "in a way that glorifies God."

Accountability begets results like nothing else on earth. Like most people, I really do not like to be accountable to others. However, I have found that I really *do like* the results that accountability pushes me to achieve.

Dr. Bill Bright, founder of Campus Crusade for Christ, gives the following exhortation on strategic giving:

> I encourage you to use the "sound mind" principle to help you determine where to invest in Christ's kingdom. Avoid emotional giving. Giving on impulse just for the sake of giving or contributing where your gifts are likely to be misused or wasted is not only poor stewardship, but is also contrary to the will of God and grieves the Spirit. Perhaps you have received requests from organizations inviting you to invest in their various projects. Carefully evaluate the worthiness of the ministry you choose and the sincerity of the people involved, and respond to the leading of the Holy Spirit.[16]

This chapter will help you select the actual investments for your Eternity Portfolio. In the search for strategic, long-term investments, we will discuss the following key questions:

➤ How many investments should I make?

➤ What types of investments should I consider?

➤ Where will I find them?

➤ How do I evaluate a specific investment?

Much of what will be covered is particularly applicable to gifts you give to a nonprofit organization—not as much to gifts made *directly* to the poor or needy. Although these investments are an important part of your portfolio, their nature does not lend itself so much to strategic evaluation and planning. However, investments in *organizations* whose mission is to reach the poor are included in the coming discussion.

HOW MANY INVESTMENTS SHOULD MY PORTFOLIO CONTAIN?

Sometimes people get caught up in random giving to just about any organization or individual who asks. Large sums of money are dispersed in tiny pieces in somewhat of a "mile wide, inch deep" philoso-phy. Strategic investments, on the other hand, take money *and* time, both of which are in limited supply.

The most effective giving strategy is one that is concentrated on a manageable number of focused organizations. I believe that most families could reasonably manage somewhere between one and five additional strategic investments (in addition to direct gifts to the poor and spontaneous onetime gifts), assuming that their church is the di-versified core of their investment strategy. Institutions such as private foundations could conceivably manage a larger number of invest-ments with the assistance of paid staff members.

You have only a limited amount of time to spend managing your Eternity Portfolio. It's probably unrealistic for you to keep abreast of the activities of dozens of different organizations. Another factor is that the most powerful combination of your money and abilities will be dedicated to ministries working in the area of your personal mis-sion. For most people, there is no way to do this with more than two or three major commitments. Finally, from a monetary standpoint, you will have more impact by making larger gifts to fewer organizations. The ability to fund specific projects or make a substantial difference in a capital campaign comes from these large gifts.

WHAT TYPES OF INVESTMENTS SHOULD I CONSIDER?

There are no hard-and-fast guidelines for choosing ministries for your Eternity Portfolio. Sometimes God uses organizations that would never have been considered strategic by anyone's definition. Some-times. That being said, there are three defining characteristics that tend to mark a project or organization for strategic, long-term success. I use these three marks as my initial screen to determine if I should in-vestigate the organization further.

1. **Inspiring leadership.** It has been said that "everything rises and falls on leadership," and that is certainly true when it

comes to investment opportunities. Effective leaders will be passionate, innovative risk takers who inspire others to follow. They may not be flamboyant or even extroverted, but the fire that burns inside for their mission will likely be evident whether you observe them in person, see them in a video, or read their words in a brochure.

2. **Focused mission.** No ministry can be all things to all people. You want to make an investment in a specific organization for a specific purpose. Make sure it has one. You are right to be skeptical of the one-man startup ministry whose mission statement is "Reaching the whole world with the gospel of Jesus Christ." No matter how admirable the goal, effective ministries start with a specific target opportunity. The vision can certainly expand as God grows the breadth and depth of the organization. But when it comes to strategic investments, look for the laser beam, not the shotgun approach.

3. **Multiplying effect.** What is the "leverage potential" of the investment? Leverage is the ability to make 1+1=3 or 2x3=100. As you evaluate investments, look for opportunities to multiply the effectiveness of your gift. For example, an individual missionary you support may have the potential to reach hundreds of individuals personally with the gospel during a given year. However, a video project on the life of Christ could impact millions of people in one year. This doesn't mean you shouldn't support the individual; however, that investment may be better classified elsewhere in the portfolio. Your strategic, personal-mission allocation should be focused on exponential growth opportunities.

I have been involved with a ministry that invites pastors from all over the United States to participate with their wives in three days of training and encouragement conducted by veteran pastors and ministry leaders from around the country. As is common in small churches, these attendee pastors are overworked and underappreciated, and many are fast approaching burnout. After three days of rest and discipling, they are ready to return home with renewed excitement for their calling. My investment in this pastor discipleship ministry is leveraged across the hundreds of individual congregations representing thousands of individuals these pastors shepherd. The lives that are changed create a multiplying effect.

WHERE DO I FIND INVESTMENT OPPORTUNITIES?

The more engaged you are in the giving process, the more God opens the door to potential investments. Sometimes this is the natural result of heightened awareness.

For us, this started in our local church. We have always supported the church financially and have often made special contributions as specific needs were identified. However, as we became more involved, other ministry opportunities arose. As God began to show us a calling in the area of discipling people in stewardship, we partnered with an organization that provided a small-group study on this subject. Working closely with the local organization leadership to coordinate the startup in our church, we became aware of the impact this small-group study was having around the country. Melissa and I decided to make an investment in the organization, and our contributions continue to this day. The point is that many times your best giving opportunities are right where you are serving.

Another important pipeline for investments is your personal relationships. Ask your friends, acquaintances at church, and especially your pastor. Chances are there are many unique ministries operating throughout your spheres of influence. Some time ago I was looking for an opportunity to be more involved in evangelism outside the United States. Within a short period of time I became aware of two strategic opportunities involving church-planting movements—one in

India, the other in Europe. God brought these to my attention through some personal relationships.

If your church is making a difference in people's lives, it is probably an incubator for new ministries. Not only might you find some great opportunities, you will have the best chance to know the leadership firsthand and be a part of the ministry. However, use caution here; startups are very tricky both in business and in ministry. The upside is that you can have a significant impact on some of tomorrow's strategic organizations as an early-stage investor. The downside is that many ministries won't make it, and choosing the "winners" is difficult. You may consider setting aside a certain portion of your portfolio just for startup organizations.

Another growing resource for those looking for investments is the Internet. A number of organizations have the specific purpose of being "clearinghouses" for giving investments. The Generous Giving Marketplace Web site at www.GGMarketplace.org is one example. Ministries that are looking for new or additional funding or planning new endeavors place proposals on the Web site. These proposals are then sorted by type of ministry, funds needed, and other search criteria. You as a donor may register with the site, entering your personal profile and describing the types of opportunities in which you might have an interest. The site will then automatically match your personal criteria to its database of proposals and show you a listing of the results. (You may also search by keyword, region, etc.) And when new proposals arrive that match your giving profile, you'll see them at the top of your welcome page each time you visit the site.

Resources such as this represent an exciting opportunity, and as Dr. Henry Blackaby has said, "you can see where God is at work and you can, with great confidence, let the Spirit of God take your heart . . . and drop it right into the middle of a timely moment in His Kingdom purposes." (More information about Generous Giving can be found in Appendix D.)

The more you pursue God's calling through your personal mission, the more opportunities you will find to invest. Giving will always be a relationship business. As your giving network expands, there will increasingly be more than you can handle. Then comes the challenge of selecting the best investments for your Eternity Portfolio.

HOW DO I EVALUATE A SPECIFIC INVESTMENT?

In the world of investing there is a concept called "due diligence." Before an investment manager buys stock in a company, he or she goes through a formal evaluation to determine how well the company compares to other investment opportunities. The company's financial statements are rigorously examined; questions are asked. Site visits to the company are performed; questions are asked. Company management presents its strategic plan; more questions are asked. The investment manager documents the results of this inquiry for future reference, and he or she finally makes the decision to invest or not to invest.

As you look to make an investment, try to determine if the organization has a strategic vision for its role in accomplishing God's plan.

You should use a similar process when making any substantial strategic investments in your Eternity Portfolio. Here's another quote from Dr. Bright:

> *Don't be afraid to ask questions. Find out the condition of the "soil." Investigate the financial soundness and integrity of the organization soliciting your support; determine what percentage of your donation will actually go to the project and whether your gift will really be used for the glory of God.*[17]

Your initial review should begin with the organization's promotional materials and financial statements. If they have a Web site, spend some time going through it. You are trying to gain an overall understanding of what the ministry is about. Begin to write down questions and start to pray that God would guide your decision.

For larger investments, try to arrange a visit to the organization so you can meet with the leadership. (Try to go as high up the chain as possible; obviously this is easier with smaller organizations or if you are a very large donor.) The *time* you invest in this evaluation process should be in direct proportion to the *resources* you are going to invest. Throughout the process you should try to measure the organization on five major criteria: purpose, people, philosophy, process, and performance.

A more extensive checklist of questions is included in Appendix C. This can help you get started in the due diligence process, but let's briefly examine these five areas.

1. Purpose. From the moment of initial contact with the ministry you should receive a clear message about their reason for existence. Get some historical information. How was the organization founded? How long ago? Is it still doing what the founder envisioned? Review the mission and values statement. Is it compelling and focused or vague and broad? Does the purpose of this ministry match up to your personal-mission priorities?

Does the organization exist merely to treat symptoms of a problem, or is it addressing root causes? Gordon MacDonald gives a great example of this using a twist on the story of the Good Samaritan. Most of us know the story: The Samaritan comes along the road to Jericho and sees a man beaten and bleeding, lying in the ditch—obviously a victim of the robbers and bandits who prey on travelers along that lonely road. The Samaritan has compassion on this man and takes him to a local inn for treatment, paying for the man's care out of his own money (Luke 10:30-37). Now what if the Good Samaritan came along that road again the following week and found another man in the same condition? And then the same thing happened the following week? At some point he should ask himself, "Should I continue paying for triage for the victims at the local inn, or should I invest in making this road a safer place?"

Similarly, as you look to make an investment, try to determine if the organization has a *strategic vision* for its role in accomplishing God's plan.

One major question you should always ask is "What makes this organization unique?" Among the hundreds of thousands of nonprofit organizations in existence there is a good bit of overlap. Is someone already doing this same ministry in the same location? If so, maybe the two could join forces to achieve greater economies of scale. When it comes to investing dollars for the kingdom, you don't want an organization that is reinventing the wheel merely to paint it their own color.

2. People. Learn early in this process that you are investing in people, not ideas or organizations. Everything rises and falls on leaders and the teams they assemble. Those you meet within the organization should be passionate about what is going on and feel their work is crucial. If the leaders or staff are merely passing time or are halfhearted in their efforts, you don't need to conduct any further investigation.

Evaluate the leaders first. What qualifications do they bring? What is their track record? After decades of investing in the kingdom, Hugh Maclellan describes his key leadership indicator this way: "Past successes are the best predictor of future successes." There will be exceptions, especially for those new to ministry, but inquire into the leaders' past work experience for clues. Do you get the sense that the head of the organization has a deep personal relationship with God and that he or she is a person on a mission? Talk to board members if possible. (Do not consider investing in a ministry that does not have a board unless it is a startup and the board is under construction.) These individuals should know more about the strategic direction of the ministry than anyone besides the CEO. Are the board members invested financially? If not, you should question from the outset whether you should be either.

Staff members are a thermometer to gauge the health of the organization. Are they busy? High-octane, leveraged organizations always have more to do than the existing staff can handle. At the same time, the staff should experience joy arising from a deep sense of purpose. Their attitudes and actions will reveal whether the lofty goals and vision of the organization are more than just snazzy marketing.

3. Philosophy. Each organization has its own way of doing things. This defining philosophy is greatly influenced by leadership but also is derived from the qualifications and personalities of the staff. Try to develop a feel for this by examining the ministry's approach to major functional areas.

Fund-raising is an example. Does the ministry see this as a necessary evil or as a way to involve people in their work? Are they building long-term partnerships or "selling a product"? Are they creative? Richard Steckel writes, "A common characteristic of excellent nonprofit organizations is the presence of innovative strategies for income generation. These organizations are 'venture seekers,' meaning that they go actively looking for ideas to generate income and often seek out private sector businesses as partners."[18]

Is the ministry always in some sort of crisis fund-raising mode (i.e., "The lights will go off if we don't receive $XX by the end of the month"), using emotional pleas to substitute for strategic, faith-based planning?

How does the leadership approach decision making? Do they implement unilateral, top-down mandates? Do leaders actively solicit planning input from staff and advisors? Note that it is one thing to have a so-called "open door" policy; it is an entirely different matter to *cultivate* a systematic process of including staff and volunteers in the strategic planning.

Finally, is there a sense of accountability, both to God and His will, and to those who invest in the ministry? Many organizations operate under the "Give us your money and we will decide how to use it best" approach, although they don't normally say it quite that way. The most strategic ministries are transparent with both their successes and their failures. They view the donor as a valuable partner and prize his wisdom, prayers, *and* financial resources. Consider it a red flag if the organization is unwilling or reluctant to provide the information you request.

4. Process. How does the organization carry out its mission? Allowing for the early stages of a new ministry, investment-quality organizations have solid infrastructure and systems in place and working effectively. Is there a written strategic business plan? How are the main activities of ministry, management, and marketing being carried out? Is the organization tracking progress and working toward identifiable goals?

Dig into the financial situation. Where does the money come from? Is more money spent on fund-raising than programs? (Don't laugh; this is sadly true more often than you would hope.) Are the proper accounting systems in place with appropriate controls? Is an audit performed each year by an independent accounting firm?

Basically you are trying to judge how effective the ministry is at its mission. Does it have the size, scope, and capacity to really push the ball forward, or will most of your investment be lost to inefficiencies within the organization? Once again, keep in mind that startup ministries will need time to ramp up. In those cases, spend as much time as possible with leadership to determine their mind-set in this area. Leaders should understand the value of building effective systems of operation.

5. Performance. Part of being a wise investment manager is periodic performance measurement. The question is basically "How has the ministry done?" Has it been effective at executing its game plan and achieving results? Evaluating performance is an ongoing part of managing your Eternity Portfolio, but you should consider it even before making the first investment. Remember, when analyzing new ministries, look at the track record of the leaders in their previous occupations. Do the same for board members. If there is no verifiable history of success, proceed with caution.

Performance is a tricky issue within nonprofits. Because of the nature of the business, it is often difficult to quantify success. The first step is for the organization to identify specific, measurable objectives. There will likely be a mixture of "activity related" goals (e.g., "identify and meet with twenty potential church planters") and "mission related" goals (e.g., "plant four hundred churches"). Both are important; however, over time, emphasis must be placed on achieving the main top-level mission goals.

An indicator of a truly strategic ministry is that each key staff person has individual, written objectives over the short and long term. Ask for examples of some goals that have been accomplished lately. How have things changed over time? Talk to people outside the organization, either indirectly related or in their target market. What is the perception of the organization? Is God glorified by the goals being accomplished as well as the way they are being accomplished?

One final note about performance: *Allow proven leaders the latitude to take risks.* Those who are trying to stay on the forefront of God's leading are sure to make some mistakes along the way. It is in the nature of exploration that "dry wells" will be dug. Although you obviously do not want to see a pattern of major failures, as long as those in leadership are accountable, they should not be prohibited from exploring new territory.

(Appendix C contains a checklist to which you will want to add your own comments and questions as you develop a feel for the due diligence process.)

MAKING THE DECISION

After much prayer and research, you are finally ready to make a decision. You have invested considerable time and energy in evaluating this particular opportunity, and now you should take a step back and look at the big picture. Ask yourself, *How well do I understand the leadership and the organization? Even if it is a great ministry, do I feel led specifically to be involved right now? Are there any red flags I can't seem to shake? What about my motives?*

Be careful that there are no prideful or self-serving motives driving your investment. You might find it helpful to identify any potential conflicts of interest between your personal benefit and the kingdom benefit. If there is some sort of personal benefit, perhaps you should give a hard second look to the whole thing. For example, are you trying to impress someone by your giving? Are you trying to create business or personal opportunities by giving? There may be times when you decide not to make an investment because you realize that the driver was really your personal gratification.

How much to give and for how long can also be tricky decisions. With established organizations, you may want to try to fund specific projects. An example would be funding the translation of Scripture into a new language or training five hundred indigenous church planters in Asia. You may not be able to fund the whole project, but you could have a part. I have found in working with successful donors that they want to make a measurable difference.

For long-term funding needs, consider establishing a certain time period for your investment. Once that time is over, the investment opportunity can be reevaluated to see if it still fits with God's will for your Eternity Portfolio. This allows the ministry to plan with no misunderstanding of your commitment.

If you're a major investor, be careful about funding too much of a ministry's operating budget. Many foundations have established rules for how they support new organizations (e.g., they will fund no more than 25 percent of the operating budget for no more than three years). If the ministry is really strategic, it should be able to attract more than one or two major investors over time.

INVITATIONS TO JOIN THE BOARD

One final area of interest when making wise investments concerns the board of directors. If you are considering a sizeable investment, do not be surprised if your due diligence process generates an offer to serve on the board of directors of the organization. As you become known to ministry leaders, your services will be in demand—and rightfully so. There is a great need for godly, strategic thinkers to assist ministries at the board level. As you consider such opportunities, keep several things in mind.

There is an old saying that the board of directors is needed for the three *W*s—wealth, wisdom, and work. My experience in working with ministry leaders is that wealth (and relationships with others who have it) tends to be the most desired of the three! However, the most effective organizations utilize the varied skills and experience of their board members. When the board is truly engaged as a body of accountability and strategic planning, the members become the best mouthpieces of the ministry. Some on the board will be great at fund-raising, others will be best at planning, still others will be good at building strategic partnerships with other organizations and individuals. All are needed.

Before you commit to serving on a board, ask questions of the ministry leader. Make sure you know what the organization will expect of you as a board member. Are you responsible for a certain amount of fund-raising? How much time will be required? Are the meetings for actual planning and strategizing, or merely for rubber-stamping the director's plans? A good understanding is critical to a good decision. Ask the hard questions now or you may find yourself in an awkward situation later, when expectations are unfulfilled on both sides. When there is a good fit, however, nothing is more fulfilling than being able to assist a ministry with your time and talents as well as your financial resources. Don't underestimate the difference you could make personally.

THE ETERNITY PORTFOLIO INVESTMENT POLICY STATEMENT

Thomas Edison once said that genius is one percent inspiration and 99 percent perspiration. Part of the perspiration comes from trying to remember the vague details of an incredible idea you worked out two weeks ago in a short burst of inspiration. The best-laid plans are *wasted* without proper documentation.

| ∞

The best-laid plans are wasted without proper documentation.

In the world of investing for institutions and high-net-worth individuals, it is common practice to work out a written agreement documenting how a portfolio will be managed. Often called an investment policy statement, this document is intended to accomplish four main goals:

1. Establish expectations for and objectives of the portfolio
2. Outline the responsibilities of all parties
3. Provide guidelines for carrying out the plan
4. Communicate benchmarks for evaluating performance

The investment policy statement serves to document the game plan and hold each party accountable for his part in the process. It should be reviewed on a regular basis to determine if changes are needed—whether in the strategy itself or in the execution. Without a well-documented plan, the investment portfolio is likely to drift from its core objectives and become less effective.

Your Eternity Portfolio strategy is no exception. Once you spend the time to work out your plan, don't waste that effort through forgetfulness or a lack of accountability. An Eternity Portfolio investment policy statement could be an integral part of your family's ongoing giving strategy. (An example of an Eternity Portfolio investment policy statement is given in Appendix B.)

The policy statement can be customized to suit your particular situation, but you will probably want to cover at least the following major points:

1. **Mission Statement.** Lay out the guiding principles for your Eternity Portfolio. This can be as simple as defining what the major focus areas will be and what type of investments are contemplated. As God works in your life over the years, expect your mission to become further refined and focused.

2. **Funding Strategy.** Document the planned method of investing in the portfolio, including amounts and timing as well as any special funding vehicles (e.g., trusts, foundations, donor-advised funds). You may also want to include some financial projections that illustrate how you arrived at the numbers.

3. **Investment Selection.** Outline the steps you've taken to evaluate potential investments. It may be helpful to include

a standard due diligence checklist such as the one shown in Appendix C.

4. **Implementation.** This section should include a list of the organizations currently supported within the portfolio and the estimated amount or percentage to be invested in each.

5. **Ongoing Monitoring.** Describe the steps that will be taken (and with what frequency) to ensure that organizations funded by the portfolio are using resources effectively to accomplish the mission.

The policy statement can be reviewed on a regular basis to make sure that it is still in alignment with your family's desires. This can be a great time for teaching children and grandchildren about the importance of giving. As they see your commitment to serving and helping others through proactive planning, that vision is increased in their young hearts. It is never too early to emphasize the importance of investing in the kingdom of God, and your annual Eternity Portfolio meeting can provide the opportunity.

Another benefit of family involvement is the opportunity to communicate your specific investing values to the next generation. This becomes very important in the case of a private foundation that transcends the death of its founder. The more your heirs understand about your giving values, the better the chance that your wishes will be continued after you are gone.

MAINTAIN ACCOUNTABILITY

We started this chapter by talking about two types of accountability. First, as stewards, we are accountable to God for our eternal investments. Rather than giving haphazardly, we should be seeking God's direction and using His wisdom to make wise investments.

Second, we should require accountability within our specific investments. No longer should we give money and then simply forget about the results. For organizations that you support with sizeable investments on an ongoing basis, schedule regular annual or semiannual meetings with leadership to stay updated. If this isn't possible, make sure you read the organization's newsletter or Web site updates and ask questions. Find out what has gone well since the last meeting and where the difficulties lie. These meetings are the perfect opportunity to offer nonfinancial support in the way of prayer or actual participation in the ministry's work.

In the case of special grants, set a follow-up meeting to discuss the results of the project. Was it an effective use of funds? How can it be done even better next time?

What you will find over time is that the most strategic ministries will communicate proactively with their investment partners. They may not know how at first, but you could be instrumental in helping define what good communication looks like. When you first get involved, offer suggestions about the kind of performance feedback you would like. Strategic organizations value donors as people, not merely as funding sources.

Remember, the word is *accountability*. Those with a long-term view for success realize that God made us to work together, not to be lone rangers. Accountability is what drives open communication, fulfilled expectations, and ultimately greater effectiveness in ministry. Settle for nothing less, and vote with your investment dollars.

CHAPTER 7
Making Wise Investments

DISCUSSION QUESTIONS

1. In the past, how have you decided which organizations to support? Do you know how effective they were in using your money?

2. Have you ever thought about your responsibility for what happens *after* you give money to an organization? Do you think you hold any responsibility for this?

3. Consider the organizations or individuals in which you are investing today. How do they measure up based on the information in this chapter?

4. Do you think it's possible that you may be called to invest in an organization that, based on earthly wisdom and prudence, just does not measure up well? Why or why not?

5. How do you find a balance between accountability for your investments and faith?

6. What is your reaction to creating an Eternity Portfolio investment policy statement? How might it help or hinder your giving?

CHAPTER 8

Passing the Baton:
A Legacy That Outlasts You

In This Chapter:

- ■ What will be your living legacy?
- ■ What about a financial legacy?
- ■ Planning your children's inheritance
- ■ Tools and techniques for advanced philanthropy

Dr. James Dobson, a psychologist and foremost expert on the family, compares the transfer of values to a relay: the most hazardous part of the competition is the handoff. At three different times during the race a sprinting athlete, at the peak of his effort in the competition, must hand the baton to the next runner, who is just getting started. If there is a collision, the race is lost. If the baton is dropped, the race is lost. Even if the baton is transferred successfully, if it is not done smoothly and efficiently, the race may be lost. This handoff must be taught and practiced over and over if the athletes are to achieve success at the highest level.

Dr. Dobson believes that in raising a Christian family, the biggest opportunity for failure is in the handoff—the transfer of values to the next generation. Although much can be learned through experience, it is parents' and teachers' intentional training that will give children the biblically based understanding they need to achieve success by God's standard.

You may already be "running well" from the perspective of your Eternity Portfolio. Or perhaps you are just getting started. If you are faithful to invest for the kingdom during this lifetime, great will be your reward. But there is something bigger—a greater reward to be had! *Start thinking now about finishing well so that you create a legacy that outlasts you.*

You have the ability to influence future generations in two specific ways so that even after you are gone from this earth you will continue to invest until the end of time. First, you can create a *living legacy* of people you have trained and influenced to create their own Eternity Portfolios. Second, you may be able to leave a *financial legacy* that will continue to make actual monetary investments after you're gone.

THE GREATEST OPPORTUNITY—A LIVING LEGACY

Many of you may think that the only way to leave a legacy is by virtue of a massive financial fortune accumulated over a lifetime. Although we will discuss opportunities to use wealth in this way, the *highest* return potential actually has very little to do with the dollars you leave. I submit that training others to be faithful managers offers a greater reward because in some way you will share in the rewards of their efforts.

God has called me to disciple others in faithful life management, and that is one of the reasons for this book. If just a fraction of those who read this catch the vision and understand through Scripture God's plan for their life and the incredible opportunity of investing in eternity, the leverage will be incredible. The same volume of leverage occurs with other teachers and pastors. And, while we are not all called to be teachers outside the home, those of us with children *are* called to be their teachers. This is where we have the best opportunity to create a living legacy as we pass along the baton of financial faithfulness. How should we go about this crucial task?[19]

A LIVING LEGACY BEGINS WITH COMMUNICATION

The transfer of values is most successful when there is early, frequent, and ongoing communication. What people learn in childhood stays with them forever. As God gave the law to Moses and the nation of Israel, He instructed them about their responsibility to the next generation:

> And these words which I command you today shall be in your
> heart. You shall teach them diligently to your children, and shall
> talk of them when you sit in your house, when you walk by the way,
> when you lie down, and when you rise up. (Deuteronomy 6:6-7)

Lay the foundation with Scripture. The central focus of all teaching should be God's Word, the Bible. Remember that only God has the power to shape a child's (or an adult's!) heart. He is responsible for life change.

When it comes to teaching faithful stewardship, focus on the verses that give instruction in that area. Help your children get a big vision for God and His plan for all of creation. Without specific instruction in this area it is very easy to develop a view of Christianity as a "Sunday thing," with associated rules and restrictions. Give your children a sense that as Christians, they are a part of God's plan—part of something much bigger than themselves.

Look for passages of Scripture that communicate God's heart for giving. Teach the connection between money given and lives changed through evangelism, discipleship, and mercy. Highlight examples of generous people throughout the Bible and as you come across them in daily living. Pray regularly that God will cultivate a heart of generosity in your children.

A LIVING LEGACY IS BUILT ON YOUR EXAMPLE

A faithful life is the best platform for teaching others. We all know that children learn by example. This is particularly true with giving; children of generous givers become generous givers, often because of the example they witnessed growing up. It has been said that you only believe as much of the Bible as you live day to day. Do not expect your children to believe what they don't see in your life. The faithful manager radiates the joy of the generous life in such a way as to be unbelievably attractive to others.

∞ |

A faithful life is the best platform for teaching others.

Tell your children about your Eternity Portfolio strategy and share stories of how you got to this point. What types of ministries make up your portfolio today? Why do you consider them strategic? Allow your children to share the experience. If you have grown children, plan special family events to gather everyone together. Share how God has blessed you and what you are doing in light of that.

You don't need to have a lot of money to do this! I heard a story recently of a man who grew up in a poor family but whose father was particularly intentional about setting an example of giving. Every two weeks as he received his paycheck, the father would gather the family together to write out the "giving checks." They would pray together, thanking God for supplying their needs once again and asking His blessing on those they supported. What an example! It left an indelible mark on those children.

The most powerful story you can share with your children is what God is doing in your life. Live and share the standard you hope they will exceed.

A LIVING LEGACY IS LEARNED BY EXPERIENCE

People learn by doing. Starting from the time they first receive an allowance or get paid for odd jobs, children should be taught to give. My own children really did not even understand why they were giving away part of their allowance, but they enjoyed putting offerings in the plate at church. (I suspect this was due not so much to their generous nature but to the fact that they had very few "wants" not provided by their parents, so the value of money was not well understood!) With proper teaching and God's grace, giving that is learned as a discipline will grow into a more developed understanding.

Kids can learn a tremendous amount through helping the poor and homeless. Consider taking some "vision trips" to urban areas or, if your budget permits, to developing countries so your children can see how most of the world's population lives. For example, over the past ten years, my business partner, Dave Polstra, has taken his family to Guatemala on numerous occasions to assist medical missionaries.

One of my major concerns for our children is that they understand how different their financial situation is from that of most people alive today. Although they may live in a middle-class world by American standards, this places them in the top fraction of a percent of the living conditions of the world at large.

Seeing and helping those less fortunate will encourage your children to have hearts of gratitude and compassion. Let them experience firsthand the joy of passing along God's blessings. They can also assist in evaluating giving opportunities. Teach them the wisdom you have gained through developing your Eternity Portfolio investment policy statement. Allow them to participate in the planning over time. I even know of a woman who hired her grandson to sort through proposals and conduct initial investigations of the ministries that were asking for funds.

For those who establish private foundations or other major financial legacies, it is even more critical to train up the next generation to be effective in making ministry investments. I have clients who include their children on the distribution committee of their foundation to involve them in the process. Do this sooner rather than later. It is not unusual for charitable foundations to stray (oftentimes drastically) from the wishes of the founding donors. Many of these problems could be avoided through proper planning and training.

CONSIDER A FINANCIAL LEGACY

It is not difficult to think of people who have made a significant financial contribution to the welfare of society through their charitable giving. Andrew Carnegie, John Rockefeller, and others come quickly to mind. Each of these individuals designed the framework of the legacy they would leave with their money. Not everyone has that opportunity (or, as Carnegie would tell you, that *burden*), but for those with significant financial resources it deserves careful consideration.

During your lifetime and after your death there are techniques that can be used to invest in your Eternity Portfolio while at the same time creating income- and estate-tax benefits. These techniques also focus and give structure to your philanthropic efforts.

When it comes to dividing the wealth you have accumulated, there are two categories of "voluntary" beneficiaries and one category of "involuntary" beneficiaries to consider. Family and charitable beneficiaries are the ones I consider voluntary. As you may have guessed, state and federal taxing authorities are the uninvited guests at the table who tend to be very well fed due to improper planning.

It is safe to say that tax savings is a huge motivator in the area of planned giving. Many people make significant gifts in years when they have a large sale of stock or a business, retirement-plan payouts, or stock-option exercises, simply because of the income-tax savings. Certainly those are not the only times to consider a major investment in your Eternity Portfolio; however, any time you anticipate an extraordinary income-tax liability you should revisit your charitable-giving plan in the interest of good stewardship. You may wish to review the discussion in chapter 4 about income taxes.

The estate and gift tax is another matter altogether. This is basically the "transfer tax" on passing an inheritance to your family (to anyone other than your spouse). Although recently there have been attempts to reduce or even eliminate this tax, it is unlikely ever to go away for good. The bottom line is that, subject to certain lifetime exemptions, you pay a tax on major transfers to your family. The tax peaks out at around 50 percent. If you are over the set limit, it costs you roughly one dollar in taxes to transfer one dollar to your children! (A $2 taxable estate times the 50 percent tax rate leaves $1 for your kids.) Keep that number in mind as we discuss leaving an inheritance for your children. If you have questions on the estate and gift tax, you'll want to contact a tax advisor.

PLANNING YOUR CHILDREN'S INHERITANCE

What is the right amount to leave my children? Should I give it to them now or after my death? Should they all inherit equally? Whole books have been written to address the issue of inheritance. There are no easy answers, so instead let me propose a series of ten questions you should consider as you seek God's will for this area of your financial life:

1. What are we trying to accomplish by bestowing this inheritance upon our children?
2. Do any of the children need an inheritance to provide care for physical or mental limitations?
3. Will the amount we plan to give be a hindrance to our children's proper character and spiritual development?
4. Do our children understand and practice faithful life management?
5. Is this inheritance going to further God's purpose in their lives?
6. Have we passed along life values as well as the inheritance?
7. Have we spent a considerable amount of time in prayer and study of Scripture to determine God's will for each child?
8. Are there educational needs of our children or grandchildren to be provided for?
9. Is it likely that this inheritance will create a dysfunctional work ethic or family dynamic?
10. Will the kingdom of God be advanced by virtue of this inheritance?

The Bible teaches that it is imperative to provide for one's family (1 Timothy 5:8) and it is good to leave an inheritance (Proverbs 13:22). However, at some level that can be overdone. When you consider the miserable success rate for people who inherit significant wealth, you begin to seriously question the level at which money can be a deadly inheritance.

For the sake of your children and grandchildren, tread cautiously.

CHARITABLE PLANNED GIVING

The simplest ways are not always best. As you consider the lifetime funding of your Eternity Portfolio, the simplest way is to give cash, as the resources are available, to the organizations you would like to benefit. But what if you would like to make a commitment to give and would like to save some taxes, but you also need to live on the income from your assets for the next twenty years? What if your only significant asset is a block of appreciated stock? What if you just sold your business and have one year to use a really large tax deduction but don't know when or where you would like to contribute that large sum?

You don't have to be a millionaire to benefit from planned giving. There are advanced giving strategies you can employ even if you only have a few thousand dollars to give. In any event, you may reach a point one day where your giving plan needs to become more sophisticated to accomplish all of your objectives. While you'll probably want to talk with a qualified financial advisor, it is helpful to have a basic understanding of the tools and techniques that are commonly used in the world of charitable "planned giving."

I have grouped the major techniques in three broad categories: outright gifts, family foundations, and partial gifts. Keep in mind that there are dozens of sophisticated techniques that can be creatively employed to achieve the best results for your situation, so consider this a primer, not an exhaustive list. Also, be aware that most large ministries and even some churches have staff members who focus on helping donors understand planned giving opportunities. Help is available if you need it.

1. Outright Gifts. As the name implies, these investments in your giving portfolio are done with no strings attached and nothing held back. Think of writing a check to your church or donating some stock to a nonprofit organization. The majority of all gifts made to charities are outright gifts of money or property. From a financial standpoint the donor is entitled to an income-tax deduction that is typically equal to the value of what is given.

EXAMPLES: OUTRIGHT GIFTS

Cash: Simplest and most time-efficient way to give, especially for smaller amounts.

Stock: Gifts of appreciated stock (publicly traded) have the added bonus of eliminating any gains in the stock without paying capital gains tax. Very good from a tax standpoint. Must have held the stock for at least a year to take advantage of this benefit. Check with the charity well ahead of time to make sure it has a brokerage account and can receive the stock.

Real Estate: Can be the gift of property or a qualified conservation easement (setting aside land for conservation purposes). Make sure the charity will accept the property before going too far down this road. Real estate can involve some tricky issues that some charities do not have the staff or inclination to deal with.

2. Family Foundations. Some time ago, one of my clients was experiencing the best year, financially, of his life. He had exercised some company stock options, and he was facing the mixed blessing of a huge income and a huge tax bill. He and his wife wanted to be able to invest a significant amount in their Eternity Portfolio but had no idea when or where. They also wanted to be able to include their children in the giving decisions over time. December 31 was fast approaching, so whatever was going to be done had to happen quickly. They decided to establish a private foundation.

The examples listed in the box on page 143 are variations on what can loosely be called the "family foundation." They are ways to receive a current income-tax deduction while delaying the actual monetary transfer to the qualified charities.

Let's consider the example of the Fleming family (Case Study 3, page 171). Todd and Emily have just sold Industrial Solutions, Inc., and in addition to $3 million in outright gifts to different organizations, they have funded their private foundation with $2 million.

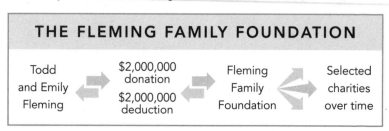

THE FLEMING FAMILY FOUNDATION

Todd and Emily Fleming → $2,000,000 donation / $2,000,000 deduction → Fleming Family Foundation → Selected charities over time

In this example the Flemings receive an immediate income-tax deduction of $2 million. Their private foundation can distribute funds to any qualified charity that they as directors choose. There is no limit as to how long the foundation can exist. Because it is a private foundation under the tax law, the Fleming Family Foundation must distribute at least 5 percent of its assets each year.

In family foundations the assets are transferred to an intermediate vehicle (see examples on page 143) and then given to the designated charities at some later point in time. This can be a very convenient tool for managing your Eternity Portfolio objectives in light of your income-tax situation. Family foundations can also be great teaching tools and can allow family members to be involved in the giving process at a higher level.

3. Partial Gifts. Let's say you have an asset that you would like to go to charity after your death. You need some additional income for living expenses, and you could really use a current income-tax deduction. Such was the situation that Rick and Barbara Cohen faced (Case Study 5, page 177).

A partial gift is one where the ministry receives some benefit either now or in the future, and the donor retains a part of the asset for personal or family use. An example is a Charitable Remainder Trust (CRT) such as the one the Cohens established. A CRT allows the donor to make a contribution of some amount in the future while receiving a current income-tax deduction *and keeping the income from the asset.*

EXAMPLES: FAMILY FOUNDATIONS

Donor-Advised Fund: A giving fund established at a brokerage firm, local community (or Christian community) foundation, or through an organization like the National Christian Foundation (www.nationalchristian.org). Also, check with your particular denomination to see if a foundation is available. Very little administration; no annual tax return filings. Most convenient way to set up a family foundation.

Private Foundation: Most flexible in terms of programs, operation, and control. However, also requires a good deal of administration in the areas of legal, accounting, and investments.

Supporting Organization: Typically established to support a particular charity. Allows the donor flexibility on timing and amount of eventual contributions to the supported organization.

The Cohens contributed $2 million to their CRT and "retained" an income interest of 5 percent. In other words, until they both are deceased, they will receive 5 percent of the trust's value each year as an income stream. In the first year that would be roughly $100,000. Whatever is left in the trust after their deaths will go to the charity. Based on their life expectancies, the current value of what the designated charity will eventually receive (as calculated using IRS tables) is $519,000. This is an estimate, but it is also the amount of tax deduction the IRS says the Cohens can claim for making the contribution. Since they retained a lifetime income from the trust, the charitable deduction is equal to the present value of the "remainder" interest. The charity only receives whatever *remains* after their deaths.

There are quite a few variations on the Charitable Remainder Trust. It is important to remember that typically the trust itself does not pay income tax. Instead, taxes are paid by the donors as the income earned within the trust is distributed to them. This makes the CRT particularly attractive if the asset being donated carries a substantial capital gain. In effect, the tax is deferred for what could be decades while the assets inside the trust continue to grow. The Cohens can decide which charity (or charities) will receive the remainder interest and can design the trust with the flexibility to change the charitable beneficiary.

THE COHEN CHARITABLE REMAINDER TRUST

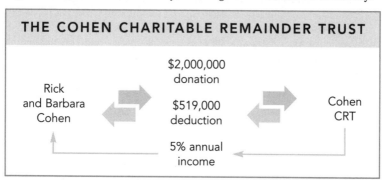

Rick and Barbara Cohen

$2,000,000 donation

$519,000 deduction

5% annual income

Cohen CRT

EXAMPLES: PARTIAL GIFTS

Charitable Remainder Trust: Donor contributes an asset and retains an income stream for life or a specific period up to twenty years. Current tax deduction is based on the present value of what the charity will eventually receive. Very effective for maximizing income-tax deduction on appreciated assets in one's estate that are planned for charity.

Charitable Gift Annuity: Donor makes a contribution directly to a charity in exchange for an annuity contract (the charity promises to pay the donor a set amount annually for life, or a certain period of years). Easier to establish and maintain than a CRT. Feasible for smaller contributions.

Charitable Lead Trust: The opposite of a CRT. Donor establishes a trust that provides an income stream to the charity for a fixed period of time. The donor's heirs are typically the beneficiaries of whatever remains at the end of the term. Used more for estate planning than income-tax planning because it decreases the value of the estate, and thus estate taxes.

PLANNING YOUR ESTATE

A great deal of charitable giving occurs at death. That probably makes sense under our old paradigm. Until you start thinking of giving as *investing* in your Eternity Portfolio, why would you start making significant donations while there is any possibility you might still need the money yourself? In fact, without the estate tax the question might become "Why would I *ever* make significant donations when there is the possibility that somebody in my family might need the money?"

I am convinced that we should prayerfully reconsider any investment we could currently make in the Eternity Portfolio that is being delayed until our death. Think for a moment about two snowballs rolling downhill. If snowball A starts one thousand feet up the mountain and snowball B starts ten feet up the mountain, which snowball will be bigger at the bottom? The one that started higher up the mountain, of course.

When I say we should be hesitant to delay funding our Eternity Portfolio, I am thinking about compounding—what Einstein called the eighth great wonder of the world. When did you start saving for retirement? Maybe you're thinking, "I wish I'd started twenty years earlier than I did." The sooner you start, the longer the rewards compound. What about leverage for the kingdom? Suppose you had a plan to pass along a message to as many people as you possibly could in your lifetime. The plan was that everyone you talked to would give the message to five of their acquaintances, who would do the same with five of their acquaintances, and so on. How many more people would you reach if you started at age forty-five as opposed to age sixty-five? sixty-five instead of eighty-five? Done properly, your investments should create an ever-expanding multiplier effect.

God is not calling everyone to give more immediately. In fact, there are two major exceptions to my premise about prayerfully reconsidering any delayed investment in the Eternity Portfolio. First is the inheritance to be passed along to your children. Obviously that would not be invested directly in your Eternity Portfolio. The second exception is what I would call your critical capital—the money you need to cover your living expenses (see chapter 5).

I realize that some people are led to give away everything they own and trust God literally to bring food and shelter to them on a daily basis. For many, however, our critical capital can be thought of as the farmland that provides our daily bread as God gives the increase. We certainly invest some of the "crop" in our Eternity Portfolio and may at some point be called to invest some or all of the land. Be willing, but be cautious. There aren't many examples in Scripture of people giving away all of their land.

> ∞ | *I am convinced that we should prayerfully reconsider any investment we could currently make in the Eternity Portfolio that is being delayed until our death.*

Even if you have money set aside in these categories during your lifetime, you will still need to do some estate planning for the amount that is likely to be left when you die. That is where many of the techniques discussed earlier can be used effectively.

One final word of caution on setting up legacy gifts to charity: It is very difficult to control how money is spent from the grave. Even with the best planning it is almost impossible to feel comfortable that a charitable entity you established at your death will still be following your wishes in even ten years, much less fifty. As Mark Twain once said, "Do your giving while you're living, so you're knowing where it's going."

YOUR LEGACY, YOUR CHOICE

You have been empowered to make a difference. The questions are "How much?" and "For how long?" Be intentional about the process. Create a living legacy and a financial legacy to make an eternal difference for the kingdom of God. The coming generations will thank you.

CHAPTER 8
Passing the Baton: A Legacy That Outlasts You

DISCUSSION QUESTIONS

1. Have you considered what sort of "giving legacy" you would like to leave behind? What would you want your family and friends to say about your life when it is over?

2. If you knew you had ten years left to live, what would you do to create the sort of legacy you described above?

3. What financial lessons are you teaching your children? Is this happening intentionally or by accident?

4. When you consider the financial legacy you might leave to your heirs, how much do you think is enough to empower them without hindering their lives?

5. Once you have decided on your children's inheritance, what will you do with the rest of your estate? What might be the best ways for you to invest more in your Eternity Portfolio?

6. What do you think about the idea that we should prayerfully reconsider any investment we could currently make in the Eternity Portfolio that is being delayed until our death? How might this idea change your estate planning?

CHAPTER 9

The Seven Golden Keys to Investing for Eternity

In This Chapter:

■ Seven principles for honoring God and creating maximum leverage through your giving

Investing is more of an art than a science. There is no one "best way" to achieve the desired results. However, though there are many methods for successful investing, a few guiding principles will take you a long way toward success no matter what the details. Concepts like proactive planning, diversification, long-term time horizon, and other boundary markers keep you on course to reach the goal.

In much the same way, there are keys to success when you're investing for eternity. Each key unlocks a part of God's heart and strategy for your Eternity Portfolio. Use the keys as a road map to direct your steps through much prayer and study of Scripture. Use them as an anvil upon which to crush improper motives, beliefs, and actions. Use them as a window through which you see more clearly God's plan for all the world and your part in it. Use the keys to unleash the incredible joy that comes from the integration of your whole being—time, talents, and treasure—into God's unique purpose for you.

THE CONVICTION PRINCIPLE

Conviction dictates action. What you believe about investing determines how you invest, how much you invest, and how long you invest. Conviction starts with understanding truth and progresses to the logical implications of that truth. It's the "values transformed to vision" formula from chapter 1.

The Eternity Portfolio is one of those progressions. It is the logical extension of biblical truth as applied to our financial resources. But *to make the jump from mere knowledge to a vision that generates results, you have to truly believe.* Let's look at three convictions that are central to the Eternity Portfolio concept:

➤ **Relationship.** Everything in the Christian life begins with a personal relationship with God through Jesus Christ. God Himself draws us into this relationship by giving us the power to believe the truth presented in the Bible. Through repentance of our sins and faith in Christ we become His children and heirs of all the promises of Scripture. *Conviction about our relationship with God is the foundation upon which our actions are based.*

➤ **Response.** A personal relationship with God brings with it the conviction that we need to respond to God's love. We are empowered by the Holy Spirit to love Him and learn through the Bible what that means.

Part of this conviction is that God has a plan for our lives— which can be found by studying Scripture—and we need to be in alignment with that plan. Jesus was referring to this plan when He said, "If you keep My commandments, you will abide in My love" (John 15:10). The apostle John wrote strong words about those who want to say that they know God but do not follow in His path: "Now by this we know that we know Him, if we keep His commandments. He who says, 'I know Him,' and does not keep His commandments, is a liar, and the truth is not in him" (1 John 2:3-4). *The faithful manager holds the strong conviction that God has given timeless truths in the Bible and that those truths form the foundation for how he or she should live.*

➤ **Rewards.** God has used the prospect of eternal rewards as a motivator throughout His recorded dealings with humankind. *The faithful manager is convinced that his or her labors on this earth* *will not be forgotten by God.* Scripture encourages this conviction: "But without faith it is impossible to please Him, for he who comes to God must believe that He is, and that He is a *rewarder* of those who diligently seek Him" (Hebrews 11:6, emphasis added). God rewards our faith in Him with eternal life, and He rewards the evidence of that faith through the work of our lives with eternal rewards. He devised the plan, and it is only by His grace that we have this prospect.

Nowhere is this demonstrated more succinctly than in two short verses describing the life of Moses. Notice the key words in the progression from relationship to response to rewards in this passage:

> *By faith Moses, when he became of age, refused to be called the son of Pharaoh's daughter, choosing rather to suffer affliction with the people of God than to enjoy the passing pleasures of sin, esteeming the reproach of Christ greater riches than the treasures in Egypt; for he looked to the reward.* (Hebrews 11:24-26)

Moses believed God and chose to live in light of that conviction in pursuit of the reward. You have to believe to catch the vision of the Eternity Portfolio as the ultimate long-term investment for your money. Faith, and thereby conviction, is a progression. As you grow in understanding God's Word, your faith grows. And true faith always proves itself through action.

The entire book of James speaks to the fact that our faith must bear fruit. As you ponder the conviction principle, think about some convictions that flow out of a proper perspective on investing in eternity. How does the Eternity Portfolio affect your outlook on work? family? greed? priorities?

THE COMMUNION PRINCIPLE

God is infinitely creative in His dealings with people. The Christian life is not about rules, formulas, and rigid structure. Just about the time you think you have His plan all figured out, He moves in another direction; always accomplishing His plan from before the foundation of the world, but in a different way than you've observed before.

Although we are given incredible wisdom in the Bible, God purposely did not fill in all the blanks. Many of the principles we understand must be applied in ways that are not specified in Scripture. We end up scratching our heads as we see God working out the *application* in vastly different ways around the world. *How am I specifically to carry out His will? Should I go about it this way or that? It seems like either way could be effective—how do I choose?*

When it comes to investing for eternity, the questions are just as complicated. Why does God call some people to give away all of their money while others are perfectly within His will when they give away only a portion? Is it possible that He exercises the faith of one woman in *giving away* the family business while directing another to *build* a business that generates funds for the kingdom? What amount should be given systematically? How does one know when to give spontaneously over and above a systematic plan? All of these questions require specific revelation of God's will in our lives. How do we get that?

The communion principle is the understanding that without ongoing, regular time spent communing with God, we cannot know His specific will for our lives. This communion starts with a regular, disciplined time alone in prayer and Bible study, but it is so much more than that. It is the state of abiding in God's presence, being quiet before Him, and listening for His direction. Sometimes that direction is given explicitly through Scripture or the godly teaching and counsel of others. However, many times it comes from the quiet voice of the Holy Spirit that guides us in the proper direction. Communion is a day by day and hour by hour activity that becomes your life over time. God desires that fellowship with you, and the revelation of His plan for you is dependent on it.

There are three specific areas of your Eternity Portfolio that will be affected by your ongoing communion with God. First, godly **motives** will stay at the forefront of your giving. In the words of Bill Bright:

Godly motives stem from a cheerful, loving heart for God. We give to please our Lord and express our love to Him. We give out of obedience to our Lord's command to lay up treasures in heaven. We give to be a channel of God's abundant resources to a desperately needy world. We give to help fulfill the Great Commission and thus help reach the world for Christ.[20]

Second, He will guide you as to the **means** of your giving. In carrying out His plan for your life, God knows exactly how much you are to invest in your Eternity Portfolio, and He will show you that over time. Finally, the **methods** of proper giving will be made clear as you commune with God. This is the "when and how" part of the equation. He will guide your planned and spontaneous giving to be most effective.

Do not fall into the trap of assuming that what God has led you to do will remain static over time. Part of the faith journey is that we don't know what the future holds. God does. Only through continual communion with Him will you be most effective in your giving.

THE CONDUCTION PRINCIPLE

When you turn on the water faucet in your house, what happens? If everything operates properly and the water bill has been paid, water streams forth in a seemingly endless supply. But what was necessary for that simple end result to occur? In most cases in America, an elaborate plan was designed to transport the water from a river, stream, or lake through miles of pipeline into your house. Along the way countless pumping and filtration systems are used to conduct that water in usable form to its final destination. Tens of thousands of people across the country spend their working lives planning, executing, and evaluating this process to further the vision of clean, usable water delivered to every home in America.

Vision leads to strategy. Just as God gives you the vision for your Eternity Portfolio, He will also lead you to the proper strategy for executing the plan. Your job is to be intentional about the plan and to use your God-given wisdom and intelligence to flesh out the details. Don't be confused into thinking that planning is unspiritual or shows a lack of trust in God. On the contrary, planning was ordained by God. Think of how He has worked throughout history. Noah was given a one-hundred-year plan for building the ark. The Israelites were given a detailed plan for worshiping God. Solomon executed a plan to build the temple. On and on the story goes. God has used short-term and long-term plans to accomplish His purposes through those who would listen and obey. The key is that they received His plan and were sensitive to His leading throughout the process of completing the plan. We must maintain a balance and make sure we don't override God's plan with our own "wisdom."

> ∞ | The faithful manager is careful to seek out God's will as to the volume (how much), the timing (when), and the direction (where) of the flow of resources.

God is the main reservoir of all material riches. *The conduction principle is God's big plan for giving: to channel those resources through faithful managers to others.* He has millions of "faucets" around the world where the "water" is needed. Your position is to be a conduit or pipeline within the cycle. This concept is expressed throughout the Bible. "Give, and it will be given to you: good measure, pressed down, shaken together, and running over will be put into your bosom. For with the same measure that you use, it will be measured back to you" (Luke 6:38). You are blessed to be a blessing. As a conduit, the faithful manager is careful to seek out God's will as to the volume (how much), the timing (when), and the direction (where) of the flow of resources.

🔥 THE COMBUSTION PRINCIPLE

As you evaluate specific investments for your Eternity Portfolio, think about the 80/20 rule: on average, for any given endeavor, 80 percent of the impact will be caused by 20 percent of the energy. You can apply this concept to almost any activity you can imagine. For example, you will find that within churches, the vast majority of the funding (80 percent or more) comes from a small percentage of the families in attendance. In business, most of the productivity comes from 20 percent or less of the employees.

This rule applies equally to your giving. Look for ministry opportunities where one little spark can lead to an explosion of results. Think of starting a massive avalanche with one little rock. The rock, however, must be pushed from a strategic place—a high place where exactly the right conditions exist to create a disproportionately large result. Your Eternity Portfolio investment is the little rock.

Looking for combustion opportunities is like looking for investment opportunities early in their life cycle. It is at that point that, if correctly identified, the opportunity will generate the highest long-term return with the smallest initial investment.

Combustion-type ministry ventures will often appear where cultural trends are converging. One of my business partners, Chris Dardaman, came across an example of this a few years ago. He was repeatedly confronted with the statistic that 85 percent of people who become Christians do so before the age of fourteen. He first struggled with the accuracy of the number, but after doing research and verifying it, he then asked why, if this was correct, churches and ministries didn't focus more on children—both for evangelism and discipleship. As a longtime teacher and promoter of stewardship within the Christian community, he was led by God to focus on teaching stewardship and financial values to children. His church, Perimeter Church in Duluth, Georgia, has started innovative stewardship programs for children and teenagers. Other churches took notice of the program and have started similar activities. As a result, thousands of children will learn to be good stewards from their youth. They will be the future business and service leaders of America, major donors to ministries, mothers and fathers modeling stewardship for *their* children.

The combustion principle means that you look for investments that result in exponential (as opposed to incremental) growth for the kingdom of God. One example would be a church-planting movement that is sweeping across a continent or country. Another would be a discipleship strategy for training and equipping pastors. Think again of the ripples created in that pond when you toss in a pebble. You have the option to invest in one person throwing pebbles or one person recruiting and training other people to throw pebbles. Which will have the most compounding impact over time?

Look for the fields that are "white for harvest" (John 4:35), and invest there. You will also have investments that are exploratory, and as we said, you will almost certainly dig some dry wells. However, when it is obvious that God is working in a certain space or time, make sure you concentrate your major dollars there. *Focus on opportunities that have the potential to explode for the kingdom.*

☈ THE COMPASSION PRINCIPLE

"But whoever has this world's goods, and sees his brother in need, and shuts up his heart from him, how does the love of God abide in him?" (1 John 3:17). When God designed the world and the people who would inhabit it, He could have set things up so that there would be no needs. No need for food. No need for clothing. No need for shelter. But for whatever reason, He allowed the system to operate so that, according to the words of Jesus, the poor would always be with us.

∞ |

Our response to the needs of the poor reflects our heart for God.

The compassion principle is this: Our response to the needs of the poor reflects our heart for God. If we really love Him, that love cannot help but show itself in love for others. How would the world look differently at the Christian community in the twenty-first century if we all invested our resources where we say our values lie? I've read stories from ancient times about how Roman emperors were motivated to set up hospitals and other institutions to care for the sick and widows and orphans because of the Christian service in that area. It wasn't so much that the Romans were concerned about the care of needy people but that they did not want the Christians alone to have such a noble reputation! Apparently the praise of the Christians was reaching jealous ears. Perhaps this is what Jesus was talking about when He said, "Let your light so shine before men, that they may see your good works and glorify your Father in heaven" (Matthew 5:16).

Is your compassion level where it needs to be? Are you actively aware of opportunities to invest in providing for the base-level needs of hurting people? The rest of the world is watching to see whether Christians really *will* help. I am convinced that when we love people at every level of society, meeting their needs from a heart of compassion and genuine concern, God uses that to show Himself to the world. You want to be a part of this.

🔑 THE CONNECTION PRINCIPLE

The intersection of your personal life mission with your giving is one of the most powerful combinations you will ever experience. I can't emphasize enough the need to connect your calling with your Eternity Portfolio. Through the process you will move beyond merely funding the work of the kingdom to the actual ministry work itself. Many times organizations need your wisdom, your time, and especially your prayers even more than your money.

It is true that where your treasure is, there your heart will be also (Matthew 6:21)—although it is not always easy to determine which comes first in that equation. We are certainly more interested in something after we invest in it. (You probably never followed a particular company's stock price until you bought some shares, for example.) However, I also believe that if the heart pulls in a given direction, the money eventually follows. This is consistent with research by the Gallup organization:

> We discovered that often people donate time and energy first,
> then make serious financial commitments to the church later. Why?

> *Because after becoming an active part of the faith community and*
> *its ministry, people not only have a vested interest in funding the*
> *work, but also truly own the ministry . . . a powerful link between*
> *giving money and giving time to a church.*[21]

Pursue this connection and take advantage of the opportunities to get involved in ministry at a deeper level. The added benefit is that you'll have a much better understanding of whether the organization is one that you should continue supporting.

The other side of the connection principle relates to connecting your children to the process of giving, which we've already discussed in detail in chapter 8. Remember to bring them in early and reinforce the connection regularly over time. Your legacy to future generations will be evidence of the connection you achieved with your own family.

THE CONSECRATION PRINCIPLE

I had the privilege recently of watching a videotaped interview of Bill and Vonette Bright. In the Brights' more than fifty years of ministry, they may have impacted more people for the cause of Christ than anyone in our time. Through Campus Crusade for Christ, the ministry Dr. Bright founded in 1952, hundreds of thousands (and probably millions) of people around the world have been touched with the love of Christ. Thousands of churches and ministries have been birthed by people formerly on staff with Campus Crusade.

In the interview Dr. Bright spoke about the "contract" he and his wife, Vonette, made with God over fifty years ago. When he left a job in business to follow God's call, they committed everything to Him. As they have lived on a modest salary, never accepting honorariums or book royalties, God has directed hundreds of millions of dollars through them to His kingdom purposes. And their needs have always been abundantly met. As Vonette Bright says, God has not been "shabby" in allowing them to enjoy many things in this life.

As I watched the video, something struck me that I haven't been able to get over. There was a glow on the Brights' faces as they talked about God as a close friend. They talked about how He had brought them along this marvelous journey and allowed them to be a part of His plan. Dr. Bright was wearing an oxygen tube during the interview and his health had declined, but still there was this aura that seemed to emanate from them. And then I realized what it was: I was watching the *overflow of a life fully consecrated to God.*

The consecration principle is this convergence of our life into the image of Christ. It is evident when we begin to understand that *everything is given over to Him* and no earthly things are really that important when compared to the joy of knowing Him.

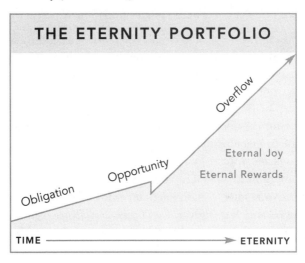

THE ETERNITY PORTFOLIO

Overflow

Opportunity

Obligation

Eternal Joy
Eternal Rewards

TIME ⟶ ETERNITY

I believe we move through a progression in our giving. As we grow, what started as an obligation moves to an opportunity and then eventually to a pure overflow of the generous life. Along the way our motivations change. The continuum might look something like the chart above. What starts as obedience gives way to a gratitude that brings a more willing offering. Next we develop an increased vision about the opportunity for eternal rewards. Finally our experience of giving and our sense of God's presence in our life manifest themselves in a joy that is not only visible but contagious. The generous life overflows.

Notice I said earlier that I *believe* this is how it works. In all honesty, I'm not there yet. I see glimpses of the overflow at times, and I see evidence of it in other people who are further along in the journey. To glorify God is our chief aim, and His glory radiates from those who have fully consecrated their lives to Him. Take notice of those who seem to be moving in this direction. Ask them about their attitudes on giving. My guess is that they have extremely generous hearts. Your Eternity Portfolio can be the start or the acceleration of this transformation in your own life.

THE ULTIMATE INVESTMENT OPPORTUNITY

I have worked with wealthy clients for years. Through their lives and experiences I've observed that although money can be a great tool, it *never* determines the level of joy or satisfaction in a person's life. Used properly, money can facilitate some great experiences. Used improperly, it can be devastating. But the fact is that true joy and happiness are there for the taking no matter whether you have much money or little. The proper alignment of God's purpose in your life with your relationships and your resources brings ultimate fulfillment.

The opportunity is before you: maximum growth investing. Really long-term investing. Guaranteed investing. Rewards beyond your imagination that last forever. Don't miss out. Don't drift through life laying up treasures on earth, seeking a reward that forever remains just over the horizon. Of the hundreds of millions of people who have ever lived, only a precious few have ever had the opportunity to impact eternity this way. You will be among the most fortunate if God uses your life and your Eternity Portfolio for His kingdom. Grasp hold and hang on tightly to that which is life indeed.

Do not lay up for yourselves treasures on earth, where moth and rust destroy and where thieves break in and steal; but lay up for yourselves treasures in heaven, where neither moth nor rust destroys and where thieves do not break in and steal. For where your treasure is, there your heart will be also. (Matthew 6:19-21)

CHAPTER 9
The Seven Golden Keys to Investing for Eternity

DISCUSSION QUESTIONS

1. Which of the seven principles (conviction, communion, conduction, combustion, compassion, connection, consecration) is the most challenging for you? Why?

2. What do you think of the idea that the intersection of your personal life mission with your giving is an unusually powerful combination (the connection principle)? How are you developing a stronger sense of your personal mission?

3. What changes might you make in your Eternity Portfolio as a result of these principles?

Appendix A
Case Studies

ABOUT THE CASE STUDIES

I've set up fictitious examples of five families who have set about developing and implementing their Eternity Portfolio strategies. Though they are from different backgrounds, family situations, and income levels, they are nonetheless united in their pursuit of the ultimate investment.

The numbers representing each family's financial situation are not meant to be exact. The nature of financial projections is that they are merely a "best guess" based on hypothetical growth rates, taxes, and earnings. The investing strategies used by each family are representative of the variety of ways people can go about this process. None is to be considered the *best* way for you and your family but is merely an idea to be explored through prayer and God's leading in your own life.

Case Study 1: Donna Rutherford—single, no children, annual income of $74,000

Case Study 2: John and Sheila Patterson—married, two children ages six and four, annual combined income of $58,000

Case Study 3: Todd and Emily Fleming—married, four children ages eight to fourteen, annual combined income varies but approximately $15 million this year due to sale of business

Case Study 4: Ben Richards—widowed, four children ages fifteen to twenty-eight, annual income of $28,000

Case Study 5: Rick and Barbara Cohen—married, one child age twenty-six, annual income ranges between $200,000 and $300,000 but due to stock-option exercise is approximately $5 million this year

DONNA RUTHERFORD—CASE 1

ETERNITY PORTFOLIO
INVESTMENT SCHEDULE

INCOME	GIVING PERCENTAGE
$0–25,000	10 %
$25,001–50,000	15 %
$50,001–100,000	25 %
$100,001–150,000	30 %
$150,001–up	50 %

Born and raised in Minneapolis, Minnesota, Donna Rutherford has two driving passions. First, as a Christian since age twelve, Donna sees her personal relationship with God as the most important thing in her life. Second, she feels that her life's mission is to be a part of global evangelism.

That's where her "real job" comes in. Just before her thirty-fifth birthday, Donna became the youngest regional vice president ever at United Package Company. Now forty-seven, she spends most of her time traveling around the world overseeing logistics at UPC's foreign operational branches. As God has developed Donna's understanding of His plan for her life, she has become a sought-after resource within the church because of her international network. Donna serves on the missions committee of her church and is on the board of an organization called Global Outreach for Asian Regions (GOFAR).

DONNA RUTHERFORD ETERNITY PORTFOLIO

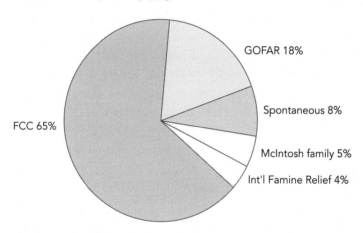

GOFAR 18%

Spontaneous 8%

McIntosh family 5%

Int'l Famine Relief 4%

FCC 65%

CURRENT YEAR ALLOCATION

LOCAL CHURCH
Fellowship Community Church. $8,000

PERSONAL MISSION
Global Outreach for Asian Regions. $2,100

POOR
International Famine Relief $500
McIntosh family $650

SPONTANEOUS
. . . . $1,000

TOTAL $12,250

Although Donna hasn't given a great deal of thought to retiring, she uses age sixty-seven in her planning. Retirement seems like a long way off, but she is currently saving 15 percent of her annual income for that purpose. Once she turns fifty-six, Donna plans to decrease annual retirement savings to 12 percent. Her goal over the next several decades is to maintain her current standard of living (adjusted for inflation) while investing an increasing amount in her Eternity Portfolio. Donna sees her current plan as a baseline for discerning God's will in this area of her life. She is sensitive to the fact that she may be led to invest some larger amounts over and above her planned giving.

Over the next thirty years Donna will invest almost $500,000 in her Eternity Portfolio based on the current projections. A comparison of her Family Portfolio (mostly retirement assets) and her Eternity

FINANCIAL PROJECTION Donna Rutherford

	Today	10 years	20 years	30 years
Donna's age	47	57	67	77
CASH FLOW				
Income				
Donna-UPC	$74,000	$99,450	$133,652	$ -
Retirement plans	-	-	-	62,926
Other investments	-	-	-	5,874
Total	**74,000**	**99,450**	**133,652**	**68,800**
Expenses				
Mtg & R.E. taxes	14,125	14,865	15,858	5,219
Income & Social Security taxes	14,169	21,290	30,870	11,726
General living	22,356	32,749	42,040	40,905
Investing				
Retirement plans	11,000	11,000	11,000	-
Other investments	100	934	5,038	-
Eternity Portfolio	12,250	18,612	28,846	10,950
Total	**74,000**	**99,450**	**133,652**	**68,800**
ASSETS				
Home	188,000	252,656	339,549	456,325
Mortgage	(134,237)	(97,041)	(22,289)	-
Retirement plans	195,040	535,654	1,205,694	1,620,351
Other investments	8,660	37,108	112,536	151,239
Total Family Portfolio	**257,463**	**728,377**	**1,635,489**	**2,227,915**

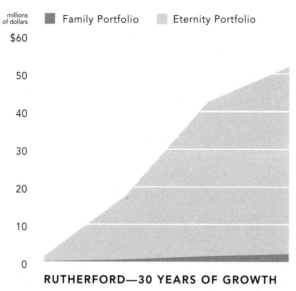

millions of dollars ■ Family Portfolio   ▨ Eternity Portfolio

RUTHERFORD—30 YEARS OF GROWTH

Portfolio over the years might look something like the graph above. Donna recognizes that based on a conservative growth rate of 7 percent on the Family Portfolio, she might accumulate as much as $2 million over thirty years. Using our earlier analogy of 10,000 percent returns in the Eternity Portfolio, we can estimate the value of her investment there as well.

JOHN AND SHEILA PATTERSON—CASE 2

Several miles west of Jacksonville, Florida, is a small community called Middleburg, where John and Sheila Patterson have just purchased their first home. They have been married for almost ten years and have two children. The oldest, Shannon, is just finishing the first grade while Jason will be starting kindergarten next year. Sheila is a legal assistant at Baker & McCoy law offices. John is the youth pastor at Middleburg First Presbyterian Church. Both of them feel called to mentor young adults in their community, especially as they are involved at church.

When it comes to saving for the future, the Pattersons have a plan.

They are diligent to invest 10 percent of their income toward retirement and intend to increase that to 15 percent at age forty-five and 20 percent at fifty-five. Each year they save 4 percent of their income for the children's college education. Although the college fund will probably not pay all the expenses for both Shannon and Jason, they hope to be able to help out with additional money when the time comes.

ETERNITY PORTFOLIO
INVESTMENT SCHEDULE

INCOME	GIVING PERCENTAGE
$0–40,000	10 %
$40,001–70,000	12 %
$70,001–100,000	18 %
$100,001–130,000	25 %
$130,001–170,000	35 %
$170,001–up	50 %

John and Sheila have served meals at a local homeless shelter with their children. They are excited about the possibility of investing financially in the shelter at some point in the future. Over their lifetime, the Pattersons expect to invest more than $1.6 million in the kingdom of God.

Even at such early ages, Shannon and Jason are starting to catch the vision as well. They are already giving part of their allowance on a regular basis.

JOHN & SHEILA PATTERSON ETERNITY PORTFOLIO

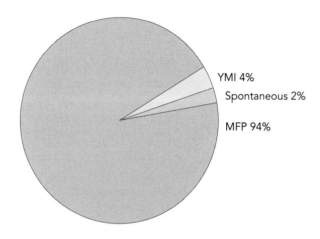

YMI 4%

Spontaneous 2%

MFP 94%

CURRENT YEAR ALLOCATION

LOCAL CHURCH

Middleburg First Presbyterian. $5,800

PERSONAL MISSION

Youth Ministries, Inc. $240

SPONTANEOUS

. . . . $120

TOTAL $6,160

FINANCIAL PROJECTION John and Sheila Patterson

	Today	10 years	20 years	30 years
John's age	31	41	51	61
Sheila's age	32	42	52	62
CASH FLOW				
Income				
John	$26,000	$34,943	$46,959	$63,108
Sheila	32,000	43,005	57,796	77,672
Total	**58,000**	**77,948**	**104,755**	**140,780**
Expenses				
Mtg & R.E. taxes	10,558	10,896	11,350	2,384
Income & Social Security taxes	8,201	12,124	18,090	25,130
General living	24,961	34,985	45,413	60,837
Investing				
Retirement plans	5,800	7,795	15,713	22,000
Other investments	-	-	-	6,156
College funding	2,320	3,118	-	-
Eternity Portfolio	6,160	9,030	14,189	24,273
Total	**58,000**	**77,948**	**104,755**	**140,780**
ASSETS				
Home	125,000	167,990	225,764	303,408
Mortgage	(118,781)	(100,525)	(63,837)	-
Retirement plans	5,800	104,490	341,318	926,079
Other investments	-	-	-	11,866
College funds	2,320	30,044	-	-
Total Family Portfolio	**14,339**	**201,999**	**503,245**	**1,241,353**

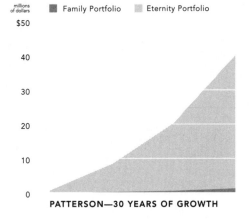

millions of dollars

■ Family Portfolio   Eternity Portfolio

$50

40

30

20

10

0

PATTERSON—30 YEARS OF GROWTH

TODD AND EMILY FLEMING—CASE 3

In 1952 Todd's father began Industrial Solutions, Inc., a manufacturer of cleaning chemicals in suburban Dallas. Todd started in the business when he was sixteen and has played a key role in its growth and expansion over the past ten years, especially after his father passed away four years ago. Industrial Solutions was sold this year for $60 million, which was roughly twice the amount that the family had invested over the years. The proceeds were split evenly between Todd and his younger sister.

Todd and his wife, Emily, have four children between the ages of eight and fourteen. In addition to running the business and raising a family, they are actively involved in fund-raising for a Christian university in Dallas. Also, they are extremely concerned about the plight of women and children around the world, particularly those in poverty-stricken areas.

As the business was being sold, many well-meaning friends encouraged Todd to retire and go into some sort of vocational ministry. Todd, however, really felt that God wanted him to start another business so that he could continue to use his business platform to the glory of God. Also, Todd and Emily both believe that he is gifted as an entrepreneur and that a new business would be a major source of additional investments in the Eternity Portfolio.

ETERNITY PORTFOLIO
INVESTMENT SCHEDULE

INCOME	GIVING PERCENTAGE
$0–40,000	10 %
$40,001–100,000	20 %
$100,001–200,000	30 %
$200,001–300,000	50 %
$300,001–up	70 %

TODD & EMILY FLEMING
ETERNITY PORTFOLIO

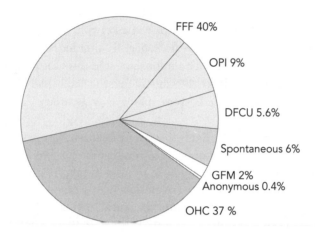

FFF 40%

OPI 9%

DFCU 5.6%

Spontaneous 6%

GFM 2%
Anonymous 0.4%

OHC 37 %

CURRENT YEAR ALLOCATION

LOCAL CHURCH
Oak Hills Church. $1,870,000

PERSONAL MISSION
Fleming Family Foundation $2,000,000
Orphan Plight, Inc. $430,000
DF Christian University $280,000

POOR
Global Foods Ministry $100,000
Anonymous gifts $20,000

SPONTANEOUS
. . . . $300,000

TOTAL $5,000,000

FINANCIAL PROJECTION Todd and Emily Fleming

	Today	10 years	20 years	30 years
Todd's age	44	54	64	74
Emily's age	42	52	62	72

CASH FLOW

Income				
Todd—Fleming Industries	$325,000	$842,966	$ -	$ -
Sale of Industrial Solutions, Inc.	30,000,000	-	-	-
Other investments	-	2,030,000	510,345	685,862
Total	**30,325,000**	**2,872,966**	**510,345**	**685,862**

Expenses				
R.E. taxes	6,200	8,332	11,198	15,049
Income & Social Security taxes	2,073,472	150,808	26,571	38,780
General living	140,328	213,826	229,334	265,930

Investing				
Fleming Industries	22,830,000	-	-	-
College funding	275,000	-	-	-
Eternity Portfolio	5,000,000	2,500,000	243,242	366,103
Total	**30,325,000**	**2,872,966**	**510,345**	**685,862**

ASSETS

Home	470,000	631,641	848,872	1,140,813
Fleming Industries	22,830,000	59,215,140	-	-
Other investments	4,987,000	7,780,184	13,141,394	17,660,934
College funds	275,000	169,052	-	-
Total Family Portfolio	**28,562,000**	**67,796,017**	**13,990,266**	**18,801,747**

The Flemings anticipate several more substantial investments in their Eternity Portfolio over and above the annual contributions. One idea they are already considering is the contribution of all of the stock in Fleming Industries to the Fleming Family Foundation. The projections above reflect this happening at age sixty. Obviously this assumes a great deal of growth over the coming years. Emily has begun to make some plans related to a crisis pregnancy center idea for the Foundation. Todd and Emily plan to allow their children to join them on the foundation's distribution committee when they reach age sixteen.

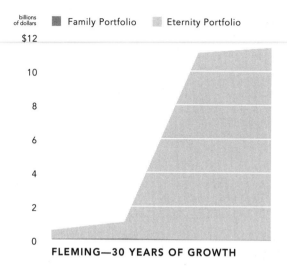

FLEMING—30 YEARS OF GROWTH

BEN RICHARDS—CASE 4

Ben Richards lives in Westin, a small community outside of Buffalo, New York, with his son, Brad (age fifteen). His older daughters, Laura and Lisa, are both married, and his youngest daughter, Abby, is away at college in Connecticut. Now fifty-seven, Ben has worked for twenty-eight years at Municipal Electric Corporation. Although of modest means, he has been saving for retirement over the years and will also receive a nice pension at age sixty-five. Ben has helped each of his children with college, although they have also taken advantage of scholarships and work-study programs.

Ben has been active in several short-term missions efforts at his church where his skills as an electrician have been particularly useful. Most of these projects have been connected with Russian orphanages that were either under construction or in need of significant repairs. He is excited about the prospect of being able to contribute even more after retirement—both financially and with his time. Ben is also starting to see gratifying results from the years of training his children. Both Laura and Lisa have great families and are faithful managers of their family resources with their husbands, and Abby is involved in the college group at a church in Connecticut.

ETERNITY PORTFOLIO
INVESTMENT SCHEDULE

INCOME	GIVING PERCENTAGE
$0–20,000	10 %
$20,001–40,000	15 %
$40,001–80,000	20 %
$80,001–up	40 %

BEN RICHARDS
ETERNITY PORTFOLIO

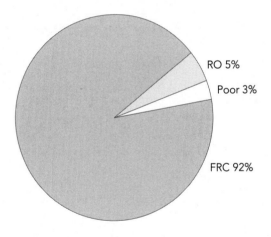

RO 5%

Poor 3%

FRC 92%

CURRENT YEAR ALLOCATION

LOCAL CHURCH
First Redeemer $2,950

PERSONAL MISSION
Russian Outreach $150

POOR
. . . . $100

TOTAL $3,200

FINANCIAL PROJECTION Ben Richards

	Today	10 years	20 years	30 years
Ben's age	57	67	77	87

CASH FLOW
Income

	Today	10 years	20 years	30 years
Ben—Municipal Electric	$28,000	$ -	$ -	$ -
Pension and Social Security	-	28,224	34,405	41,940
Other investments	-	3,030	4,072	5,472
Total	**28,000**	**31,254**	**38,477**	**47,412**

Expenses

Mtg & R.E. taxes	3,344	3,533	993	1,335
Income and Social Security taxes	5,191	4,777	6,250	8,393
General living	16,265	19,256	26,462	31,202

Investing

Eternity Portfolio	3,200	3,688	4,772	6,482
Total	**28,000**	**31,254**	**38,477**	**47,412**

ASSETS

Home	82,000	110,201	148,101	199,036
Mortgage	(22,643)	(5,201)	-	-
Other investments	42,800	78,017	104,848	140,907
Total Family Portfolio	**102,157**	**183,017**	**252,949**	**339,943**

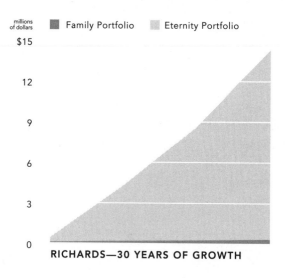

millions of dollars

■ Family Portfolio ■ Eternity Portfolio

$15

12

9

6

3

0

RICHARDS—30 YEARS OF GROWTH

RICK AND BARBARA COHEN—CASE 5

Rick and Barbara Cohen have been investing for years. In addition to sizeable retirement accounts, Rick has roughly $8 million in company stock options and Barbara owns one half of Cohen & Braden, CPAs. Even though they have been investing in their Eternity Portfolio for some time, the Cohens feel that now is the time to really increase their giving. This year they will exercise and sell $5 million in stock options to start the process. Of that amount, $2 million will be used to fund a Charitable Remainder Trust, $1.7 million will be invested in their Eternity Portfolio, and the balance will go to pay income taxes. The Cohens plan to use the annual payments from the Charitable Remainder Trust to fund a portion of their retirement-income needs.

ETERNITY PORTFOLIO
INVESTMENT SCHEDULE

INCOME   GIVING PERCENTAGE

Income	Giving Percentage
$0–100,000	10 %
$100,001–200,000	15 %
$200,001–300,000	20 %
$300,001–up	30 %

Rick has been involved in church-planting efforts for several years now and believes that a significant portion of their portfolio should be devoted to this purpose. Barbara considers her gifts to be in the area of helping people become more faithful with their time, abilities, and resources. Her favorite investment, Christian Life Managers, empowers people to explore their God-given life purpose in order to make a difference for the kingdom of God. The Cohens also desire to make a major investment in homeless ministries focused in the San Francisco Bay area, where they live. They intend to accomplish this over the next few years using the money invested in their Donor-Advised Fund, which was set up as part of their current year's Eternity Portfolio investment (see chart below).

RICK & BARBARA COHEN ETERNITY PORTFOLIO

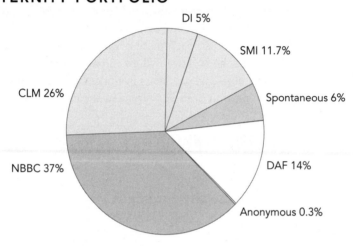

DI 5%
SMI 11.7%
CLM 26%
Spontaneous 6%
NBBC 37%
DAF 14%
Anonymous 0.3%

CURRENT YEAR ALLOCATION

LOCAL CHURCH
North Bay Baptist Church $628,000

PERSONAL MISSION
Christian Life Managers $450,000
Disciple International $87,000
Strategic Missions, Inc. $200,000

POOR
Donor-Advised Fund $230,000
Anonymous gifts $5,000

SPONTANEOUS
. . . . $100,000

TOTAL $1,700,000

Although Rick is "retiring" to be more involved in ministry, Barbara intends to work at her CPA firm for at least three more years. At that time they are considering another major investment in the Eternity Portfolio.

FINANCIAL PROJECTION Rick And Barbara Cohen

	Today	10 years	20 years	30 years
Rick's age	60	70	80	90
Barbara's age	55	65	75	85
CASH FLOW				
Income				
Rick – Applied Spectra, Inc.	$132,000	$ -	$ -	$ -
Barb – Cohen & Braden, CPAs	167,500	-	-	-
Rick – Stock Option Exercise	5,000,000	-	-	-
Retirement plans	-	74,886	100,641	135,254
Charitable Remainder Trust	-	175,817	214,320	261,255
Total	**5,299,500**	**250,703**	**314,961**	**396,509**
Expenses				
R.E. taxes	18,000	24,190	32,510	43,691
Income & Social Security taxes	1,407,621	45,256	57,005	70,955
General living	128,954	146,116	175,958	207,910
Investing				
Retirement plans	44,925	-	-	-
Charitable Remainder Trust	2,000,000	-	-	-
Eternity Portfolio	1,700,000	35,141	49,488	73,953
Total	**5,299,500**	**250,703**	**314,961**	**396,509**
ASSETS				
Home	684,000	919,239	1,235,380	1,660,248
ASI stock options	3,200,000	-	-	-
Cohen & Braden, CPAs	642,000	-	-	-
Retirement plans	1,210,000	1,928,327	2,591,510	3,482,773
Charitable Remainder Trust	2,000,000	3,586,675	4,372,136	5,329,610
Total Family Portfolio	**7,736,000**	**6,434,241**	**8,199,026**	**10,472,631**

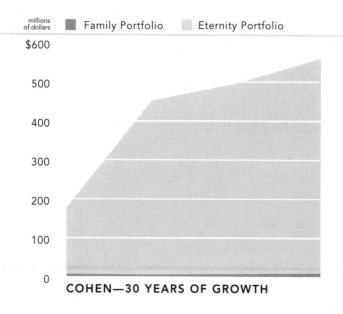

millions of dollars ■ Family Portfolio ▓ Eternity Portfolio

$600

500

400

300

200

100

0

COHEN—30 YEARS OF GROWTH

Appendix B
Eternity Portfolio Policy Statement

This is one family's version of an investment policy statement. While yours doesn't need to look exactly like this or be this formal, this example will give you an idea of where to start and what areas you should cover.

THE JOHNSON FAMILY
ETERNITY PORTFOLIO
Investment Policy Statement
January 1, _____

I. INTRODUCTION

The purpose of this Eternity Portfolio investment policy statement is to establish a clear understanding of the goals, objectives, and management policies of the Johnson Family Eternity Portfolio ("portfolio"). The investment policy statement will:

➤ Serve as a written summary of our family's *current* philosophy for making eternal investments and provide a reference for future discussion.

➤ Create the framework for wise giving through proactive planning and documentation in the following areas:

➤ Determining how much to give each year (funding strategy)

➤ Designating broad categories for giving (asset allocation)

➤ Choosing the organizations to support (investment selection process)

➤ Keeping up with the sponsored organizations (monitoring and review)

This investment policy statement will be reviewed at least annually to ensure that it continues to reflect the family's God-given desires for the portfolio. Brad and Karen Johnson are the acting investment managers ("managers") of the portfolio.

II. MISSION STATEMENT

The Johnson Family Eternity Portfolio is intended to glorify God and serve His purposes by investing in strategic opportunities as described in the following statement:

We feel that God has called us specifically to fund and be involved with ministries that are engaged in creative and high-yield evangelism strategies with an intentional process for long-term discipling. Church-planting movements are a major part of this effort. We also desire to be involved in organizations that focus on disciplining in the areas of faithful life management. Furthering the vision of Christ's church in life stewardship is a driving force within our personal mission.

—Brad and Karen Johnson

Organizations of all sizes will be considered for the portfolio; however, we have a preference for opportunities to make a bigger impact in smaller organizations. That being said, we do not intend to fund more than 15 percent of any organization's annual operating budget.

The concept of leverage is important in our giving. We are actively looking for investments that demonstrate the probability of leveraged results across geographic areas, denominations, and people groups.

III. FUNDING STRATEGY

We intend to invest $35,000 cash this year in the portfolio. Current and future giving is based on, but not limited to, the exponential generosity strategy shown below.

ETERNITY PORTFOLIO
INVESTMENT SCHEDULE

INCOME	GIVING PERCENTAGE
$0–40,000	10 %
$40,001–80,000	15 %
$80,001–120,000	25 %
$120,001–up	30 %

IV. TAX POLICY

The standing policy of the portfolio is that all investments are made only to organizations exempt from U.S. income tax under section 501(c)(3) of the Internal Revenue Code. This is in keeping with a stewardship goal of minimizing income taxes. However, specific opportunities sometimes create the need to make nondeductible contributions. Direct gifts to the poor are one example of this. This tax policy is not intended to limit investments so much as it is to focus them for optimal effectiveness.

V. ASSET ALLOCATION

The following graphs show our Christian mission broken out into the three broad categories of investments for the portfolio. These categories were chosen as representative of the biblical priorities set forth in the great commandments (Matthew 22:37-39), the great commission (Matthew 28:18-20), and the overwhelming amount of Scripture on

THE CHRISTIAN MISSION ALLOCATION

giving to the poor and needy. The main categories have been further subdivided to reflect the different subsectors of available investments. The Johnson Eternity Portfolio is intended to be invested in each of the three major classes—evangelism, discipleship, and mercy, but with a strategic personal mission focus in church planting and Christian education.

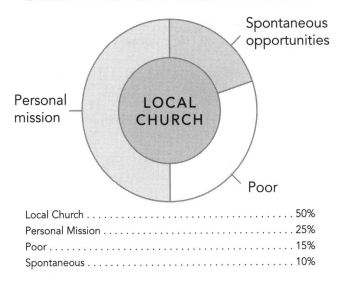

**JOHNSON FAMILY
ETERNITY PORTFOLIO TARGET ALLOCATION**

Spontaneous opportunities

Personal mission

LOCAL CHURCH

Poor

Local Church	50%
Personal Mission	25%
Poor	15%
Spontaneous	10%

Each of the investment organizations operates in one or more of the three phases of the Christian mission (evangelism, discipleship, mercy). For example, our investment in the local church is probably equally weighted between the three.

Note that the allocation of 10 percent to the "spontaneous" category is intended to be invested as God leads in any of the other areas (local church, personal mission, poor). Historically, this has been used for onetime grants or special opportunities to minister to the poor.

The allocation of 15 percent to the poor is not our only investment in that category, as several other ministries supported within the portfolio are actively involved in that area. However, this is the part of our portfolio where we are directly involved with the poor around us. It can consist of anonymous cash gifts to individuals, providing food or medical services, and so forth.

VI. INVESTMENT SELECTION PROCESS

Organizations are brought to our attention in any of a number of ways. Often we are introduced to ministry leaders through personal relationships. The decision of whether or not to make an investment is guided by prayer and the following process:

1. Set up an initial interview with the head of the organization (or as high up as possible)

2. Visit the site, if possible, to look at facilities and talk with personnel

3. Review the most recent financial statements, budgets, projections, and marketing materials/proposals

4. Network with other contacts who may know the key leaders of the organization

5. Gain an understanding of what the organization does, how it does it, and what challenges and opportunities it faces

During this process we are trying to answer concrete as well as intangible questions about the ministry, its leaders, its purpose, and its potential effectiveness. Some of these questions are listed in our separate due diligence checklist (see Appendix C). These criteria are not rigid but are part of the process used to make sound judgments as to which of potentially thousands of organizations to support.

VII. IMPLEMENTATION

BRAD & KAREN JOHNSON
ETERNITY PORTFOLIO

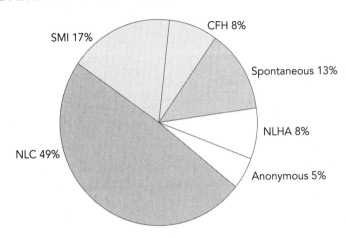

CURRENT YEAR ALLOCATION

LOCAL CHURCH
North Lake Church $17,000

PERSONAL MISSION
Christian Financial Hope $3,000
Strategic Missions, Inc. $6,000

POOR
N.L. Homeless Association $2,800
Anonymous gifts $1,600

SPONTANEOUS
. . . . $4,600

TOTAL $35,000

VIII. MONITORING AND REVIEW

Organizations are expected to provide regular communications regarding the status of the ministry and current developments. We review the financial and strategy updates to stay abreast of the organization's progress. If doubts arise, the investment selection process is restarted with a review of the previous answers to the due diligence checklist.

Ministries can be removed from the portfolio for a number of reasons, including the following:

- Strategy shift in the overall allocation of the portfolio
- Integrity lapses within the organization
- A pattern of inefficient use of funds
- Failure to be effective in reaching ministry objectives
- Lack of focused vision/sense of purpose
- Persistent failure to provide information on a timely basis
- Ministry not open to or ignores constructive feedback

IX. ADOPTION

We the managers of the Johnson Family Eternity Portfolio do hereby approve and adopt this investment policy statement.

Brad Johnson _____Date _____

Karen Johnson _____Date _____

Appendix C
Due Diligence Checklist

When you're considering whether to fund a specific organization, there are many issues to consider. Here's how to get started:

➤ Review marketing/collateral information such as the organization's Web site, brochures, annual report, and presentations.

➤ If possible, conduct a site visit or vision trip to examine the operation firsthand.

➤ For large gifts, meet with leadership to better understand who they are and where the organization is headed.

➤ Either through a face-to-face meeting, telephone call, or collateral information, try to get a sense for the following:

I. ORGANIZATIONAL ASSESSMENT

A. PURPOSE

1. What is the mission of the organization? What specifically are the major problems/issues it is trying to address?
2. What makes this organization unique?

3. What is the scope of the organization's activities (local, regional, global, country-specific)?
4. Are there well-developed, high-level goals that have been established to mark progress and give guidance to staff and donors?

B. PEOPLE

1. How well do I know the leadership? Are they visionary? capable of leading? passionate about the mission? Do they value relationships?
2. What qualifications do those in leadership have?
3. Does the board of directors represent a cross section of skills and qualifications needed to successfully guide an organization of this type? Are the board members investing financially in the ministry in a significant way?
4. Do the staff members understand the organization's mission and exhibit a genuine concern for their area of ministry? Do they seem content and motivated?

C. PHILOSOPHY

1. How receptive is the organization to feedback and questions? Do leaders appear transparent about problems, successes, and failures?
2. How are donors treated? Is there a demonstrated accountability for the faithful use of funds? How are volunteers recruited, trained, and utilized?
3. Does the ministry seek to create leveraged results for the kingdom (i.e., multiplication)?
4. Do there seem to be any "integrity fault lines" running through the different aspects of the ministry? its fund-raising? programs? communications?

D. PROCESS

1. Is there a written strategic plan for the ministry?
2. As it carries out its mission, how is the organization perceived within the community?
3. What are some of the new initiatives or activities the organization is undertaking?
4. Where does the financial support come from? A small group of major donors or a broad audience?
5. Are there audited financial statements?
6. Does the organization appear to be staffed appropriately to execute the mission?

E. PERFORMANCE

1. How does the organization measure its progress toward accomplishing the mission? Are there specific targets and objectives for the leadership as well as staff within the organization?
2. Does the organization communicate regularly and effectively with the donors? What is the frequency?
3. Is the organization accomplishing its mission?

II. PROJECT ASSESSMENT

These questions apply if a specific project is being considered for funding. Review the project proposal.

A. ORGANIZATIONAL FIT

1. Does this particular project address one of the core objectives of the ministry? In other words, is it part of a focused, concentrated effort toward accomplishing the organization's purpose, or does it go outside of core competencies and mission?
2. Is this project or activity already being conducted successfully by another organization, and if so, are there reasons to duplicate?
3. How much of the funding is already committed?

B. PROJECT REVIEW

1. Is this a onetime investment for a project that will become a self-sustaining activity?
2. Other than in the area of funding, where are the faith hurdles? In other words, where must God supernaturally create the results for the project to be successful?
3. Do the financial projections seem reasonable? Are they too optimistic? Do they leave anything out? Is there a plan for contingencies?
4. Are there specific, measurable objectives to be accomplished?
5. How will progress be reported?

III. FINAL ASSESSMENT

1. Have I (we) spent sufficient time seeking God's will through prayer, Bible study, and wise counsel? Do I (we) have any wrong motives or conflicts of interest that should prevent this investment?
2. Assuming all indications are positive, are there any nagging questions or concerns that should be resolved?
3. Whether or not this appears to be a great opportunity, do I (we) feel specifically led to be involved at this time?

Appendix D

Resources

∞

BOOKS:

FINANCIAL STEWARDSHIP

Your Money Counts, Howard Dayton
How to Manage Your Money, Larry Burkett
Money, Possessions, and Eternity, Randy Alcorn (revised edition)
God and Your Stuff, Wesley K. Willmer
Whose Money Is It Anyway? John MacArthur
Master Your Money, Ron Blue
Cost Effective College, Gordon Wadsworth
Debt Free Living, Larry Burkett
The World's Easiest Guide to Finances, Larry Burkett
Sound Mind Investing, Austin Pryor

ETERNITY AND ETERNAL REWARDS

Your Eternal Reward, Erwin W. Lutzer
In Light of Eternity, Randy Alcorn

Eternity, Dr. Joseph M. Stowell
The Law of Rewards, Randy Alcorn

GIVING

The Treasure Principle, Randy Alcorn
Generous Living, Ron Blue
Giving and Tithing, Larry Burkett
The Generosity Factor, Ken Blanchard and S. Truett Cathy
Secrets of the Generous Life, Gordon MacDonald

WEB SITES:

The Eternity Portfolio On-line: www.EternityPortfolio.com
Generous Giving: www.GenerousGiving.org
Generous Giving Marketplace: www.GGMarketplace.org
Crown Financial Ministries: www.crown.org
Guidestar: www.guidestar.com
MinistryWatch: www.ministrywatch.org
National Christian Foundation: www.nationalchristian.com
New Tithing Group: www.newtithing.org

OTHER MATERIALS:

Crown Financial Ministries Small Group Bible Study (also a special edition for those entrusted with wealth)

Stott on Stewardship: Ten Principles of Christian Giving, Dr. John R. W. Stott (Generous Giving)

Divine Mathematics: How One Plus One Equals Three in the Kingdom, Selwyn Hughes (Generous Giving)

ENDNOTES

[1] Dr. John F. MacArthur, Jr., *The MacArthur New Testament Commentary on Matthew 1–7* (Chicago: Moody Press, 1985), 425.

[2] Erwin Lutzer, *Your Eternal Reward* (Chicago: Moody Press, 1998), 38.

[3] As quoted in Douglas M. Lawson, *Give to Live* (La Jolla, Calif.: ALTI Publications, 1991), 81.

[4] Lutzer, *Your Eternal Reward*, 21.

[5] Rev. Thomas Gouge, *Riches Increased by Giving* (Harrisonburg, Va.: Sprinkle Publications, 1992), 44.

[6] Randy Alcorn, *In Light of Eternity* (Colorado Springs: WaterBrook Press, 1999), 125.

[7] Dr. John F. MacArthur, Jr., *The MacArthur New Testament Commentary on 1 Timothy* (Chicago: Moody Press, 1985), 285.

[8] Jonathan Edwards, *Heaven—A World of Love* (Amityville, N.Y.: Calvary Press Publishing, 1999), 57.

[9] MacArthur, Jr., *The MacArthur New Testament Commentary on Matthew 1–7*, 411.

[10] Rev. Samuel Harris, *The Scriptural Plan of Benevolence* (New York: American Tract Society, circa 1850), 25.

[11] Rev. Parsons Cooke, *The Divine Law of Beneficence* (New York: American Tract Society, circa 1850), 43.

[12] Harris, *The Scriptural Plan of Benevolence*, 11.

[13] Andrew Carnegie, *The Gospel of Wealth* (Bedford, Mass.: Applewood Books, 1998), 15.

[14] Cooke, *The Divine Law of Beneficence*, 79.

[15] Ibid., 80.

[16] Bill Bright, *How You Can Experience the Adventure of Giving* (Orlando, Fla.: New Life Publications, 2002), 19.

[17] Ibid., 20.

[18] Richard Steckel and Jennifer Lehman, *In Search of America's Best Nonprofits* (San Francisco: Jossey-Bass Publishers, 1997), 54.

[19] I am grateful to Howard Dayton and Larry Burkett for helping shape some of my thoughts on teaching financial principles to children.

[20] Bill Bright, *The Christian and Giving (Ten Basic Steps Toward Christian Maturity, Step 8)* (Orlando, Fla.: New Life Publications, 2002), 17.

[21] George Barna, *How to Increase Giving in Your Church* (Ventura, Calif.: Regal Books, 1997), 50.

ABOUT GENEROUS GIVING

Studies show that U.S. Christians give proportionately less today than they did during the Great Depression.

Generous Giving is a nonprofit educational ministry that seeks to encourage givers of all income levels—as well as ministry leaders, pastors, teachers, and professional advisors—to fully understand and embrace what it means to live generously according to God's Word and Christ's example. Generous Giving was launched in 2000 by the Maclellan Foundation, a fifty-year leader in Christian grant making, to stir a renewed commitment to generosity among Christians. *Our mission is to motivate followers of Christ toward greater biblical generosity.* We envision the hearts and minds of God's people transformed for revolutionary giving.

We offer an array of practical tools such as books, study guides, quarterly briefings, e-newsletters, and an exhaustive on-line library of news articles, statistics, Bible studies, streaming media, and Scriptures and sermons on generosity. We also sponsor large and small gatherings, in a safe environment free from the pressure of solicitation, where givers can hear inspiring stories of men and women who have experienced financial freedom through the joy of giving.

We also host the Generous Giving Marketplace, a Web site that brings givers and ministry opportunities together (www.GGMarketplace.org). This is a one-of-a-kind classified listing of hundreds of funding opportunities posted by scores of Christian ministries.

See that you also excel in this grace of giving.
2 Corinthians 8:7, NIV

For more information about Generous Giving, we invite you to contact:

Experience the Joy.

Generous Giving, Inc.
One Fountain Square, Suite 501
Chattanooga, TN 37402
(423) 755-2399
www.GenerousGiving.org

More Generous Giving books from Tyndale . . .

SECRETS OF THE GENEROUS LIFE
Gordon MacDonald

ISBN 0-8423-7385-3

In this book of inspiring and thought-provoking reflections, best-selling author Gordon MacDonald reveals the secrets of joyful, generous living and explains why a generous lifestyle is such an accurate measure of one's soul.

THE LAW OF REWARDS
Randy Alcorn

ISBN 0-8423-8106-6

From the best-selling author of *The Treasure Principle* comes this inspirational and motivational book on God's incentive program. Discover the source of true riches and lasting joy as you refocus your priorities and take a new look at the real route to happiness.

Generous Giving is not a publicly supported charity and does not solicit funds or allow solicitation at any of its events.